# A Guide to Trade Credit Insurance

# A Guide to Trade Credit Insurance

By the International Credit Insurance & Surety Association

ICISA
INTERNATIONAL CREDIT INSURANCE & SURETY ASSOCIATION

ANTHEM PRESS

Anthem Press
An imprint of Wimbledon Publishing Company
*www.anthempress.com*

This edition first published in UK and USA 2015
by ANTHEM PRESS
75–76 Blackfriars Road, London SE1 8HA, UK
or PO Box 9779, London SW19 7ZG, UK
and
244 Madison Ave #116, New York, NY 10016, USA



*British Library Cataloguing-in-Publication Data*
A catalogue record for this book is available from the British Library.

*Library of Congress Cataloging-in-Publication Data*
A catalog record for this book has been requested.

ISBN-13: 978 1 78308 482 1 (Hbk)
ISBN-10: 1 78308 482 0 (Hbk)

This title is also available as an ebook.

# Table of Contents

# Foreword

I am very pleased on the occasion of the 85th Anniversary of the International Credit Insurance and Surety Association (ICISA) that it is marked with the presentation of this book, *A Guide to Trade Credit Insurance*.

As a technician and manager in the credit insurance industry I very much enjoyed reading this book and I can recommend it to anyone interested in trade credit insurance, as it provides a clear introduction and explanation of the trade credit insurance product.

I would very much like to congratulate and thank all the authors, editors and reviewers for their hard work in making this book such a success. I would also like to thank Willem Bongaarts and Edward Verhey at the ICISA Secretariat for managing the process on behalf of the Association towards its successful launch. It takes real dedication to make such a project happen and all concerned should be justly proud of this achievement and its readers be appreciative of the excellent result.

I wish you pleasant reading.

Jim Davidson
*President ICISA*

# Introduction

In 2007 the International Credit Insurance and Surety Association (ICISA) published the first edition of the Catalogue of Credit Insurance Terminology in order to clarify terms used in credit insurance for the benefit of anyone who is not familiar with them. The catalogue became a success and was translated into French, German, Italian, Spanish and Japanese. It forms the basis of the expanded 'Glossary of trade credit terminology' in this volume.

In 2010 the Management Committee of ICISA approved the production of an ICISA book on trade credit insurance. The aim of this book is to have an industry-wide reference manual for the sector and to better position the trade credit insurance industry.

The Credit Insurance Committee of ICISA identified a Project Team, which selected the industry experts in their field as authors and editors for the book. The result of this collaborative effort by the Project Team describes the 'lifeline' of the credit insurance product, from the initial application stage to the expiration phase of the policy, including practical use aspects for credit managers.

This book is not meant to be a comprehensive encyclopaedia of all possible variations in trade credit insurance, but offers compact information on the history of trade, the need for protection against trade credit risks and solutions offered by credit insurance providers.

The focus is on short term credit, including whole turnover policies and single risk policies.

The following authors have contributed to the content of the book through essays or by editing chapters. They work(ed) for the companies mentioned, when they wrote their contribution or edited the content. The book was edited by Martin van der Hoek (Coface).

| | |
|---|---|
| Miguel Aguirre | Coface |
| Peter Aitken | Atradius |
| Felipe Buhigas | Mapfre |
| Herbert Daniel | Zurich |
| Martin Da Re | Coface |
| Doris Egli | Scor |
| Markus Eugster | Catlin Re |
| Louis Habib-Deloncle | Garant |
| Markus Heizmann | PartnerRe |
| Martin van der Hoek | Coface |
| Werner Jäger | Hannover Re |
| Joe Ketzner | Euler Hermes |
| René Mul | Atradius |
| Joachim Osinski | Atradius |
| Rossella Pappalardo | Sace BT |
| Irmgard Paul | Prisma |
| Joost van Steen | Coface |

Incidental repetition of information occurs in order to maintain the structure of the chapters.

The ICISA Yearbook may provide the reader with additional information. This companion document may be found on the ICISA website (www.icisa.org).

Trade Credit Insurance is more than insurance and I hope you will discover this by reading this book written by various experts from ICISA member companies. For more information on Trade

Credit Insurance or how it can facilitate your trade, I recommend contacting one of the ICISA member companies.

I wish you pleasant reading.

Robert Nijhout
*Executive Director ICISA*

# Disclaimer

Information provided in this Book has been prepared as a convenience to the reader. Reasonable efforts have been used in collecting, preparing and providing quality information, but no warranty is made or guaranteed about the accuracy, completeness, or adequacy of these. Under no circumstances shall ICISA or its member companies be liable for any direct, indirect, special, punitive or consequential damages that arise out of or are in connection with errors, inaccuracies, omissions or defects of any content in this book, even if ICISA, its member companies or an authorized representative of any of these has been advised of the possibility of such damages.

This Book provides a description of terminology commonly used in trade credit insurance and describes mechanics and methodologies that may be used by the trade credit insurance industry. The Book does not warrant or represent that the descriptions given are legal definitions. This Book is not the particular view of any individual insurer or reinsurer and does not represent nor intend to describe either the general or specific underwriting or risk management style, mechanics, methodology or policy terms and conditions of any individual insurer or reinsurer. No rights can be drawn from the descriptions in this

Book, and these descriptions shall not modify, alter, clarify or otherwise provide meaning to terms that may be used in any trade credit or political risk insurance policy, or to any operational methods that may be employed by any individual insurer or reinsurer. Each individual insurer and reinsurer is independently responsible for determining how its business shall operate.

CHAPTER 1

# What Is Trade?

*In order to write a book on Trade Credit Insurance there should be a clarification of the wording of the subject. This book starts with short descriptions of Trade and Trade Credit Insurance.*

Today, the term 'trade' is used for transactions that involve multiple parties participating in the voluntary negotiation and exchange of one's goods and services for desired goods and services of another party. The advent of money as a medium of exchange has allowed trade to be conducted in a manner that is much simpler and effective compared to earlier forms of trade, such as bartering, which is the act of trading goods and services between two or more parties without the use of money.

Trade has evolved considerably over time; however, the basic elements of buying and selling in some form of a market have not changed, because ultimately, trade still involves transferring the ownership of goods from one person or entity to another.

## ABSOLUTE AND COMPARATIVE ADVANTAGE

One of the major benefits of trade was described by Adam Smith in 'An Inquiry into the Nature and Causes of the Wealth of Nations'. First published in 1776, this theory states that free market economies are more productive and beneficial to their societies and that nations can only benefit from one another if free trade is practised. The main argument here is that a country can produce goods or services at a lower cost per unit than the cost at which another country produces that good or service.

Later in 1817, David Ricardo described in his publication 'On the Principles of Political Economy and Taxation' how two countries, or any kind of different parties, can both benefit from trade if, in the absence of trade, they have different relative costs for producing the same goods. David Ricardo illustrated the importance of comparative advantage in an example involving the trade of cloth and wine between England and Portugal in order to describe how productivity levels dictate the patterns of trade.

Whilst profitable gains from absolute advantage may only be beneficial to one of the trading parties, comparative advantage explains that every country can gain from trade.

International trade allows economies to use their resources – whether labour, technology or capital – more efficiently. Because countries have different assets and natural resources, some countries may produce the same goods more efficiently and therefore sell it more cheaply than other countries. In other words, trade determines a country's import and export structure.

The conclusion drawn is that free trade exists due to specialization of skills and division of labour in areas where different areas have the highest comparative advantage in the production of a number of tradable commodities. However, since productivity levels do not remain constant but are rather influenced by a learning process based on experience, dynamic effects of specialization on comparative advantage should not be neglected.

## TRADING GLOBALLY TO INCREASE EFFICIENCY

Trading between different regions or countries has been common for thousands of years. International trade is the exchange of goods and services across borders. If a country cannot efficiently produce an item, it can obtain the item by trading with another country that can. Without international trade, nations would be limited to those goods or services that can only be produced or provided within their own borders.

Basically, free trade has to lead to international division of labour and therefore to interdependence between countries. This type of trade gives rise to a world economy in which prices arising out of supply and demand affect and are affected by global events.

International trade not only results in increased efficiency due to comparative advantage but also allows countries to participate in a global economy, encouraging the opportunity of foreign investments. As a result and in theory, economies can grow more efficiently and become more competitive economically. In principle, countries where foreign investments are made show a rise of employment levels which eventually leads to an increase in their gross domestic product. On the other hand, investors benefit from market expansion and growth; thus translating into higher revenues.

In this sense, there is a causal connection between economic growth and international trade as the specialization of countries on its 'core competencies' and the exchange of goods traded internationally increase global productivity and the variety of products available for consumption.

## TRADE CHRONOLOGY

In times where nations did not exist, international trade meant trading over long distances. In this period of history, trade was very similar to today's concept of international trade.

Trading between different parties likely goes back to prehistoric times when goods and services were bartered before the beginning of civilization. Polished stone axes, ornaments of amber and shell, and copper or bronze implements, for example, have been assumed to be primitive valuables and have been used to infer incipient social ranking since the Neolithic Age (from 9500 BC).

In ancient times, Arabian nomads carried out long distance trade by camel caravans to the Far East bringing spice and silk to Europe. The Egyptians travelled through the Red Sea trading spices from Arabia.

In the Middle Ages it is worth mentioning the Abbasid Caliphs who used Siraf, Alexandria, Aden and Damietta as ports to travel into India as well as into Chang'an, the Chinese capital of the Tang dynasty that was regarded as the eastern depot of the Silk Road to China for the purposes of trade.

It was also during the Late Middle Ages that the Hanseatic League secured trading privileges and market rights in England for goods from the League's trading cities in 1157.

In early modern times the Portuguese established trade routes from Europe to India and Japan and Vasco da Gama became one of the major figures in the history of international trade. It was also in this Age of Discovery, in 1602, that the Dutch East India Company was established to carry out trade in Asia.

As time went on, the development of international trade continued to progress. More and more countries were involved in trading networks and eventually in the 19th century the first trade agreements were signed between different nations. The Free Trade Agreement sealed between Britain and France in 1860 set off successive agreements between other countries in Europe.

The further liberalization of international trade may be characterized by the formation of Free Trading Areas (FTA), customs unions, common markets or economic integrated regions.

In 1958 the European Economic Community (EEC) was established with a common commercial policy, and thus this was the first example of both a common and a single market in the 20th century. Although in earlier centuries there had been predecessors such as the United States of America and the Latin Monetary Union, the EEC additionally had a customs union.

## THE WORLD TRADE ORGANIZATION

In 1947 following the end of World War II, 23 countries agreed to the General Agreement on Tariffs and Trade (GATT) to guarantee free trade.

In 1955 the World Trade Organization (WTO) officially replaced the GATT. The WTO is an organization that offers a stable system for governments to achieve their goals in trade by supervising and liberalizing global trade.

The main functions of the WTO consist of the implementation, administration and operation of the voted agreements. It serves as a platform for negotiations and settlement of disputes and provides assistance for developing, least developed and low-income countries to adjust to WTO policies and regulations.

The WTO cooperates closely with the two other components of the 'Bretton Woods' system, the IMF and the World Bank. More information on the WTO is available on www.wto.org.

## FAIR TRADE

Fair Trade, started as an alternative to free trade, focused on dialogue, solidarity and transparency with the objective of promoting greater equity in international trade. It contributes to sustainable development by offering better trading conditions to and securing the rights of companies in developing and less developed countries. Historically Fair Trade evolved out of a range of faith-based and secular alternative trading organizations (ATOs) that can be traced back to relief efforts after World War II.

## CONCLUSION

International trade has tripled since the year 2000. This significant growth is primarily due to various political and technological developments of our age. The political rise of countries like Brazil,

Russia, India and China has influenced worldwide markets. At the same time, technological changes such as the Internet have decreased information asymmetry and lowered costs for logistic services accelerating the development of global trade.

Organizations like the WTO have helped the liberalization and deregulation of international markets. In summary, international trade opens up the opportunity for specialization and more efficient use of resources and therefore has the potential to maximize a country's capacity to produce and acquire goods.

CHAPTER 2

# What Is Trade Credit Insurance?

*No matter how transparent an international trade transaction may be, it is not completed until payment is received. Businesses usually trade on open credit terms as an alternative payment instead of immediate cash payment to provide time for buyers to generate revenue from sales to pay for the delivery of goods and the performance of work or services. For those businesses this 'account receivable' is unsecured invested capital due to the commercial or political risk of non-payment or any payment delay.*

## HISTORY, NATURE AND IMPORTANCE OF TRADE CREDIT INSURANCE

The first hints of modern trade credit insurance came at the end of the 18th century. In 1766, a Prussian professor Wurms proposed to authorities a type of insurance to cover maritime risks in order to reduce losses caused to merchants.

In 1839, an Italian, Bonajuto Paris Sanguinetti, published his work: 'Essai d'une nouvelle théorie pour appliquer le système des assurances aux dommages des faillites' ('Essay of a New Theory to Apply Insurance to the Losses Caused by Bankruptcies'). He is considered the founder of Credit Insurance in a defined approach.

In 1849 the Banque Mallet Frères et Cie in France was the first to cover trade credit risks, an example quickly followed by four other banks in Paris. After an initial great success these banks had to stop their credit insurance activities because of difficulties with the strict separation between banking and insurance. By supporting overdue buyers of their insureds, they sustained many losses and decided to cease writing credit insurance in France.

The *credit line* is generally considered to have originated in the United Kingdom, where property and casualty insurers were already covering credit business in the middle of the 19th century, and from where credit insurance spread to continental Europe around the end of the 19th century.

The oldest specialized credit insurer still operating today was founded in 1893 in the USA, but credit insurance never really took hold in the USA during the next 100 years. Only since about the turn of the millennium has credit insurance in the USA been undergoing a noticeable upswing, albeit still low in comparison to Europe.

In 1918 England was the first country to develop, a public (government-backed) guarantee scheme to cover transactional risks. This example was followed by Belgium in 1921, Denmark in 1922, the Netherlands in 1923 and many other countries in the years to come. At that time some emblematic companies were created, being still active today, namely, Hermes founded in Germany in 1917, Trade Indemnity in UK in 1918 and NCM in the Netherlands in 1925. Four years later, SFAC was introduced in France and Compagnie Belge d´Assurance Credit in Belgium. Each of these companies considered trade credit insurance as a new activity and were able to overcome the 1929 economic crisis.

For many decades and until today European countries have been generating by far the largest part of the global credit insurance premium volume. In the 1990s credit insurance spread rapidly around the world with high growth rates, though in some regions from a low baseline. However, there are still some regions where trade credit insurance is virtually unknown, if it exists at all, such as Africa outside South Africa, in the Arab world, in large parts of Asia, some countries in South America and in most of Eastern Europe. Even in the established markets of Europe the market penetration lies between only about 10% and 25% (measured in terms of potential market volume), depending on the country and the definition of insurable markets. The total value of the underlying business covered world-wide is more than a thousand billion (trillion) euros and the global annual premium volume is estimated at around €6 billion – with a rising trend. Since 1990 a strong concentration process has led to the formation of large corporate groups with global operations – alongside a several independent providers – the three market leaders account for a share of about 80% world-wide. Nearly all private credit insurers are members of the International Credit Insurance & Surety Association (ICISA).

## DEFINITION

Trade credit insurance (also named delcredere insurance, credit insurance, business credit insurance or export credit insurance) is the insurance product that businesses purchase to protect themselves against the risk that a buyer defaults on a payment obligation. By purchasing a trade credit insurance policy, businesses are able to extend insured credits to their customers and simultaneously reduce the risk of payment default.

The insurer is the company providing insurance cover that underwrites a risk of payment default, whereas the insured is the party purchasing an insurance policy that assumes the rights and obligations of the policy.

Trade credit insurance is usually classified into *commercial* and *political* risks.

*Commercial* risk is associated with the insured's customers and their ability to pay for the delivery of goods and or performance of works or services provided to the seller; i.e. the insured.

*Political* risk refers to the buyer's country and includes losses arising from political events such as (outbreak of) war, promulgation of laws, embargos or other governmental measures that either limit or interfere with the trade of the free disposal of the contractual consideration to which the insured is entitled.

Whereas for decades the political export credit risk was borne almost exclusively by the public sector Export Credit Agencies (ECAs), since the turn of the millennium most private credit insurers have been offering both commercial domestic and international cover and also political cover, often in a single (comprehensive) policy.

Trade credit insurance is based on the principle of a bilateral relationship between the insured and the insurance company where both parties agree to obligations towards one another. To distinguish trade credits from purely financial credits not related to an underlying trade transaction, receivables are only insurable if they relate to goods supplied, services rendered or work performed under a contract (trade credit) in the course of the normal business operations of the party to whom the receivables are due. It covers the payment risk resulting from the insured's delivery of goods and performance of works or services to their customers on open credit terms. In other words, trade credit insurance is purchased by business entities to insure their accounts receivable from losses due to unpaid invoices as a result of protracted default, insolvency or bankruptcy of buyers.

The insurer compensates the insured for losses of insured receivables from a portfolio of buyers that occur during the insurance period of insurance. In exchange for insurance cover, the insurer charges the insured a premium amount. The premium is usually calculated as a percentage of all outstanding receivables, the total of credit limits underwritten or the insured's insurable turnover. Theoretically, the premium rate used for calculating the premium should reflect the average credit risk of the insured portfolio of buyers.

Trade credit insurance policies provide for maximum liabilities which restrict the total compensation payable by the insurer for losses from political or commercial risks occurring within one single policy year. These amounts are limited usually to either a fixed amount or to a multiple of the annual premium paid during the same policy year.

Trade credit insurance compensates the insured for losses arising out of the payment risk of other companies but not of private individuals.

Trade credit insurance policies often combine domestic and export sales with an indemnity level up to 90 per cent. Receivables shall be insured if and insofar as the insurer has evaluated the creditworthiness of the insured's buyers and stipulated a sum insured and a credit limit for each buyer. By investigating the financial position of prospective buyers, the insurer evaluates whether or not particular transactions constitute acceptable risks.

In order to perform the assessment of risks, the insurer uses an extensive information network with trade reference and collection agencies, banks and rating agencies just to name a few. In case of aggravation of risk, the insurer has the right to reduce or cancel credit limits of a certain buyer.

Apart from credit limits assessed and issued by the insurer, trade credit insurance policies may allow cover under a discretionary limit. For those buyers insured under the discretionary limit, the granting of credit must typically be justified on the basis of written information provided by an approved credit agency and/or a positive payment history where the buyer has obtained goods or services from the insured for which the buyer has made due and proper payment. In this case, the insurer will issue a policy with a limit of discretion (i.e. insureds that invoice buyers up to a designated, fixed limit do not need to have these amounts previously approved by the insurer). If a specific credit limit (usually in excess of the discretionary limit) is required, the insured will have to submit a specific credit limit application to the insurer. This process involves the insurer's risk assessment of underwriting information (credit reports, financials, management accounts, etc.).

In addition, in cases of buyers who default in payment, insurers also conduct recoveries through a network of solicitors and collecting agents.

Insurance cover is available on either a single-transaction or buyer portfolio basis.

In most policies, the insurer is provided with the right of subrogation that grants the insurer the contractual right to collect compensation directly from the buyer who has failed, or take legal actions against him. In such cases, all claims of the insured against the buyer and all ancillary rights are subrogated to the insurer in the amount of compensation paid.

Exclusions from coverage include failure to comply with policy obligations such as the non-reporting of adverse information regarding the financial standing of a specific buyer, non-payment of premium or non-payment due to disputes.

## BENEFITS OF TRADE CREDIT INSURANCE

It has become essential to businesses to evaluate and manage future risks in challenging economic times. It is estimated that, depending on the type of a company, 20%–40% of a company's assets are in the form of trade receivables and it is very difficult for a company to predict which buyer will default on payment. The costs of non-payment can be considerable to a business. Whilst loss rates vary in different industrial sectors and countries, every business is susceptible to non-payment of a trade debt or insolvency.

Concerning this issue, insurance companies play an important role in risk management by offering several benefits. The main benefit of trade credit insurance consists in the management and in the protection of a company's accounts receivables by compensating the insured in the event of non-payment.

In addition, trade credit insurance also helps an insured compete more effectively. Credit terms offered to buyers have become an important component of competitive strategy. Credit insurance allows the insured to gain competitive advantages through extended open terms, higher credit limit values and expansion into new markets.

In summary, further benefits of trade credit insurance are:

- profit and cash flow liquidity protection;
- risk avoidance by focusing on credit control upon problem accounts;
- information services when making commercial decisions to promote sales growth;
- access to the financial history and credit worthiness of potential buyers;
- enhancement of credit management procedures as cash flow improves and 'days sales outstanding' (DSO) are reduced;
- borrowings and other lines of finance are made more accessible due to increased bank security;
- bad debt reserves can be reduced therefore freeing up capital;
- longer terms of payment can be offered.

# CHAPTER 3

# Product Types

*There are various ways to categorize the trade credit insurance products ('policies') that credit insurance companies offer to the market.*

## 1. LEVEL OF SELECTION

One of the ways to classify policies is according to the level of risk selection that the trade credit insurance allows. To what extent and under what conditions these product types are actually available in general or in a particular situation will depend on the individual trade credit insurer's own offering strategy. Generally speaking: the better the spread of risk and the lower the possibility of anti-selection, the higher the probability of acceptance by the trade credit insurer and the lower the relative costs (= premium) for the insured.

***a) Whole turnover***

This is the most traditional policy form that covers the entire business-to-business turnover of the insured company, that is, all business transactions with all their buyers (both current buyers and future buyers). From the point of view of the trade credit insurer, this ensures a maximum spread of the risk over buyers and buyer countries.

***b) Selected part of the turnover***

As long as the risk-to-premium profile remains acceptable, trade credit insurers are usually prepared to cover a selected part of the insured's turnover. For example: only the company's domestic sales, only their export business or only a specific division or a particular product line (such as cover for the delivery of printers, but not for the sale of spare parts or for the maintenance and service contracts).

***c) Selected buyers***

Cover can also be restricted to the turnover made with a number of selected buyers. This selection may be on fairly objective criteria such as cover only for buyers on which the outstanding amount exceeds a pre-agreed level ('Datum line') or cover only for the insured's largest x number of buyers ('Key account' or 'Key buyer'). Such selection may also be on less objective criteria, covering a number of buyers that have been explicitly chosen by the insured.

***d) Single buyer***

In this case the insurance covers all sales transactions with one specific buyer only. An even further level of selection is single contract cover, where the policy covers only one single transaction with a single buyer.

## CUSTOMER TYPE OR DISTRIBUTION CHANNEL

Another way of classifying the various insurance products would be by type of customer for which the product has been developed.

Next to their more traditional policies for the mid-market segment, most larger trade credit insurers also have products tailored to the (Micro) SME (Small and Medium-sized Enterprise) segment and the multinationals segment. Entry-level policies for the (Micro) SME segment may typically have simplified terms and conditions, a minimum of administrative burden and a basic service support from the trade credit insurer. Policies for the global enterprises are usually multi-currency, multi-language programmes tailored to the organizational structure and demands of the multinational, serviced by dedicated account teams.

Trade credit insurers may also adapt their products to make them more suitable or attractive for (potential) customers in specific trade sectors. Examples could be a trade credit insurance policy for the construction sector or for the recruitment sector, where additional features are added to the policy that better capture the typical or unique trade characteristics of the sector.

Trade credit insurers may have trade credit insurance products adapted to the distribution channels they are employing. This can result in further simplified or standardized products that are easier to sell by non-specialist brokers, agents or bank sales staff. Or the policies may have been adapted to be bundled with other types of business insurance.

Large companies with a well-established credit management process may not be interested in a traditional whole turnover policy, but may be only looking for support of their credit management with insurance for the situation where their losses exceed the frequency or severity level that they can cope with themselves. Excess-of-loss or catastrophe cover policies provide such cover. These policies only pay out an indemnification above a considerable first loss amount that the company has to bear itself. Such policies normally also give a high level of autonomy to the company in setting limits for their buyers. That is why this type of policy is suitable only for insureds with excellent credit management that meets the credit insurer's strict requirements and why the company's written credit management procedure is usually an integral part of the policy. Any breach of the agreed credit management procedures can cost the insured his insurance cover.

## BASIS OF THE INSURANCE

Trade credit insurance policies may be distinguished by the coverage basis of the insurance.

In a risk attaching policy cover is attached to contracts where the shipment dates of the goods or the performance of the services occur within the insurance period, that is to say the commencement of coverage is determined by the point at which the risk itself commences during the policy's lifetime. Cover continues after the expiry of the policy, i.e. even if the actual loss occurs after the insurance period the insurer still is liable.

In a losses-occurring policy the insurer's liability is determined by the date of the cause of loss within the insurance period. If the date of loss doesn't fall within the insurance period, the loss is not covered.

An example to illustrate the difference between these two insurance types:

- The policy start date is 1 January 2011 and the policy expiry date is 31 December 2011.
- The policy is not renewed.
- During this insurance period, the customer ships goods on:
  1) 10 September 2011 (invoice due date 10 December 2011),
  2) 15 October 2011 (invoice due date 15 January 2012),
  3) 20 January 2012 (invoice due date 20 March 2012).
- The buyer becomes insolvent on 28 February 2012.

In a risk attaching policy, the credit insurer is liable for losses regarding the shipments 1) and 2), which were done during the insurance period, but not for shipment 3), which was not shipped during the policy contract.

In a losses occurring policy, the credit insurer is not liable for the loss regarding any of these shipments, because the date of the insolvency (the cause of loss) does not occur during the insurance period.

Almost all credit insurance policies belong to either of these two types. Whether a particular trade credit insurer offers risk attaching policies or losses occurring policies usually depends on what is customary or typical for their home market. Larger trade credit insurers usually offer both types.

For completeness' sake, it is worth mentioning the so-called claims made policy. This policy type covers applications for indemnifications made during the policy's lifetime. This type is less common in credit insurance.

CHAPTER 4

# Risk Types

*Trade credit insurance covers insured against the risk of non-payment by their buyers for goods and services delivered on credit terms. The types of risk causing the non-payment loss which trade credit insurers most commonly cover are insolvency, protracted default and political risks.*

## COVERED RISKS AND CAUSES OF LOSS

Insolvency can be defined as the institution of a judicial or administrative procedure whereby the assets and affairs of a legal entity (the buyer) are made subject to control or supervision by the court or a person or body appointed by the court or by law, for the purpose of reorganization or liquidation of the buyer or of the rescheduling, settlement or suspension of payment of its debts. The precise forms, names and terms of these insolvency procedures vary per country and jurisdiction. Insolvency may in shorter terms be described as the buyer's officially recognized inability to pay its creditors.

Terms and conditions of insolvency cover may vary somewhat from insurer to insurer. For example, it is sometimes required that the debt is lodged in the insolvent estate and acknowledged, before the insurer proceeds to indemnify the insured's loss.

Also, the policy's insolvency cover definition may include events that the trade credit insurer deems comparable to insolvency, for example, an extrajudicial settlement with all or the majority of the buyer's creditors or the execution of a court judgement that fails to satisfy the amount owing or the situation that starting an insolvency procedure against the buyer will have no cost effective result due to the buyer's weak financial position.

The typical character of this cause of loss is that the loss for the insured is definite as soon as the buyer's insolvency has materialized, although the eventual amount of the loss may not be fully known and is depending on the chances of distribution of funds from the insolvent estate. As a consequence, normally all outstanding amounts on the buyer, whether they are already due or not at the date of insolvency, are indemnified under the trade credit insurance policy at once.

**Protracted default** is the situation in which a buyer fails to pay the contractual debt within a period (the waiting period) that is pre-defined in the trade credit insurance policy. This waiting period is usually calculated from the due date of the debt or from the date the insured submits the claim and/or hands over the collection of the unpaid debt. The typical length of the waiting period is 4 to 6 months. So for example, if an invoice is due on 15 March, with a 6 month waiting period calculated from the original due date, there is a situation of protracted default if this invoice remains unpaid on 15 September – assuming that the buyer is not in a formal state of insolvency at that moment in time.

Protracted default may be described as the failure by a buyer to pay the contractual debt within a pre-defined period calculated from the due date or extended due date of the debt. In fact, protracted default may be seen as offering a bridge for the insured between two possible outcomes of the situation: either the buyer eventually pays his debts or he becomes insolvent. Particularly in jurisdictions where insolvency procedures are lengthy or slow, this protracted default cover is a valuable feature of the trade credit insurance policy.

Contrary to insolvency cover, under protracted default cover the unpaid trade debts become claimable as and when the waiting period expires for each of them.

**Political risk** cover in trade credit insurance includes a whole range of risks of which the common denominator is that they are beyond the scope of an individual buyer or fall outside the individual buyer's responsibility. Political risks are loss-causing events related to the country of the buyer. Hence they are also called country risks.

The precise scope of the political risk cover depends on the terms of the individual insurer's policy wording – for example, some credit insurers may extend political risk cover to events occurring outside the seller's or buyer's country (a cover of risks caused by so called 'third countries') – but in general political risk cover includes all or a selection of the following occurrences:

- payment-stops decreed by the government;
- transfer delays, foreign currency shortages and inconvertibility of currency;
- violence such as war, martial law, civil unrest, insurrection, rebellion, revolution or riot;
- cancellation or non-renewal of import or export licenses, import embargo;
- confiscation of goods by the government;
- governmental measures that prevent the performance of a trade contract.

Furthermore, any trade contract directly concluded with public buyers such as states, ministries, governmental departments and so on is often included contained under political risk cover.

As with protracted default cover, there is usually a waiting period before a claim may be submitted for political risk cover, normally starting on the due date of the invoice and varying between 4 to 6 months.

Additional premium will be charged in case the trade insurance policy includes political risk cover.

Political risk cover can also protect bank's financing and pre-financing obligations. The bank may be included in the policy as an assignee and receive the indemnification in case of a covered loss. Trade credit insurance protection partly mitigates that risk and triggers a capital release.

## EXCLUDED RISK AND LOSSES

Apart from listing the types of risks and losses that they cover, trade credit insurance policies also describe the risks and losses that are not covered by the insurance.

In case a non-payment of the trade debt is related to a dispute between seller and buyer, trade credit insurers deny liability for the loss, until and to the extent that the dispute is resolved in favour of the insured and the buyer perseveres in non-payment of the final amount that parties agreed.

If non-payment is caused by the **insured's own failure** to satisfactorily perform the contract or to comply with the law or to obtain the necessary licenses, the loss cannot be claimed under the policy.

Usually, **intercompany trade transactions** are excluded from the policy. The reason for this is that the insured and the buyer have an interest or control in each other and this could lead to manipulative payments to the detriment of the insurer and could have a negative influence on recovery actions.

Furthermore, trade transactions with **private individuals** (e.g. non-business) are excluded from the policy since trade credit insurance is a typical business-to-business insurance.

Finally, **interest** or **penalties** that the insured may be entitled to (contractually or otherwise) do not qualify for indemnification.

## PRE-CREDIT RISKS

The buyer may become insolvent before the goods are delivered or may not be able to receive the ordered goods.

Political circumstances (war, a ban on import into the buyer's country, a ban on export to the buyer's country) make it impossible to deliver correctly.

*Force majeure* (a natural disaster) prevents the supply of goods.

The trade credit insurer withdraws cover before the goods have been delivered and instructs the insured to sell the goods elsewhere.

Thus, the loss sustained by the insured may relate to the costs made in vain, or to the lower price in case of resale of the goods. These pre-credit risk causes of loss may be added to the policy conditions as an extension of the insurance beyond credit risk only.

In the event the insured is in default to supply the ordered goods in time or otherwise according to the contract, this occurrence is caused by the insured itself, and a policy with pre-credit risk cover will not cover the losses arising in such circumstances.

Wherever in this chapter 'delivery' is mentioned, this shall also mean either 'shipment' or 'rendering of services'.

## WHAT ARE THE PARAMETERS OF THE INSURED PRE-CREDIT RISK?

The preferences of the insured, as well as the willingness of the insurer, will determine the extent of the pre-credit risk that can be insured.

Important considerations include:

For the insured:

Is the insured aware of the pre-credit risk and wants to insure this risk? Does the insured believe it will be easy to sell the goods elsewhere, when the buyer cannot or does not want to accept the goods at delivery? The insured will be less concerned about the possible need for re-sale for standard than for goods made according to the specifications of the buyer.

For the insurer:

Is the insurer prepared to extend cover of a trade credit insurance policy by adding the cover of pre-credit risk? The willingness will depend on the trade sector of the insured, the nature of the goods to be supplied, the length of the pre-credit period (between acceptance of the order and delivery) and the resale possibilities of the non-accepted goods. Does the insurer want to cover the insured's liability when there is a breach of contract caused by the insured not delivering the goods because the insurer instructed that shipment be held?

The individual policy conditions for the pre-credit risk cover should address the above mentioned considerations.

## DIFFERENT TYPES OF PRE-CREDIT RISK

All these questions and circumstances lead to the development of different sorts of pre-credit risk cover, which may include one or more of the following characteristics or elements.

- ***Incidental cover or whole turnover insurance***

The insured's wishes may lead to the cover of the pre-credit risk of only single transactions or under special circumstances. The policy gives a standard cover for the credit risk. Although it causes an anti-selection which is not favourable, the insurer may be prepared to provide for this incidental cover in exchange of an appropriate premium. However, the insurer shall prefer to cover pre-credit risks for the whole insured turnover.

- ***With or without discretionary limits***

Some insurers stipulate that for the insurance of pre-credit risks only credit limits established by them will apply. Other insurers are prepared to provide this cover under discretionary limits.

- ***Binding contracts/Pending orders***

In some countries pre-credit risks are only insured in case of medium or long term credits (longer than 180 days after delivery) and the delivery of capital goods. In other countries the pre-credit risk may be insured in case of short term credit (up to 180 days after delivery) and in case of delivery of consumer goods, raw materials and semi-manufactured goods.

In countries where the cover of pre-credit risk is not common, policy clauses were developed that provide for maintained cover after a reduction or withdrawal of the credit limit, when binding contracts or pending orders may oblige the insured to deliver. Under these clauses cover depends on the insurer's incidental approval for delivery.

- ***Only pre-credit risk cover in case of insolvency***

Some insurers confine the pre-credit risk cover to the cases of the buyer's insolvency before delivery of goods or completion of the services. This implies that other causes of loss are excluded from the cover. Other insurers do not apply this restriction.

- ***Protracted default***

In case the goods to be delivered cannot be accepted by the buyer within the waiting period for protracted default, which in case of pre-credit risk cover is deemed to start upon expiry of the agreed term for delivery, some insurers provide for cover of the pre-credit risk, even when the buyer is not insolvent. In addition, pre-credit insurance can protect against political risks before delivery, for example when the country of the buyer prevents the delivery of the goods to the buyer.

- ***Political risks***

When political risks are insured under the conditions of pre-credit risk cover, it should be made clear when the waiting period for the insurance of these risks will start (upon expiry of the agreed term for delivery), and which political risks are included or excluded from cover, comparable to the cover of the credit risks.

- ***Act of State/Fait du Prince***

Measures or legislation by the government of the insured's country (also called Act of State/Fait du Prince) are excluded from pre-credit risk cover in almost all sorts of credit insurance. This means that when after the acceptance of an order and before delivery of the goods the government of the insured's country does not allow the shipment of the goods to the buyer's country (refusal of an export licence, a boycott of the buyer's country) the pre-credit risk cover will not lead to indemnification.

- ***Consequential losses of liabilities***

Every insured may decide to do business without insurance. Nevertheless, when pre-credit risks are insured, the insurer may be able to provide valuable insight to the insured, which may reduce the risk. The insurer may instruct the insured to stop the production of goods or not to deliver the goods to the buyer, because the insurer has doubts whether the buyer will be able to pay due to decreased creditworthiness or imminent insolvency. The insurer can also withdraw the cover of credit risks for future deliveries to the buyer's country.

In these cases the insured has the choice:

- to follow the insurer's instructions in order not to endanger the policy's indemnification of the costs already made; or
- to deliver the goods at its own risk and for its own account, because of fears of a breach of contract default notice by the buyer.

If the insured follows the insurer's instructions not to ship, it is possible that the buyer will hold the insured liable for breach of contract. The insured's own suppliers may do likewise because of the insured's own non-acceptance of goods that may have already been ordered prior to receiving the insurer's instruction. Consequential losses and liabilities because of breach of contract are not always included in the conditions for pre-credit risk cover.

## TECHNICAL ASPECTS OF PRE-CREDIT RISK COVER

Each trade credit insurer has specific conditions and systems for the insurance of pre-credit risks. Yet there are some general aspects which deserve attention in case of pre-credit risk cover.

***- Declaration of orders, invoices or outstanding balances***

The premium charged for the insurance of *credit* risks is based on two important aspects:

- the declaration of invoices (turnover) per month, quarter or year
- the declaration of balances outstanding at the end of each month

Should *pre-credit* risk cover be included in the policy, these risks would be insured for no additional premium if no separate provision was made for paying premium on purchase orders even if these orders do not result in deliveries or lead to deliveries after the expiry of the policy.

Therefore, a separate declaration of these purchase orders and a separate premium charge is one means by which the insurer can be compensated for the additional coverage it provides. Alternatively, an increase of premium for the credit risk, i.e. a surcharge for the inclusion of pre-credit risk cover, is another method.

However, insurers still need to determine a methodology for the amount of premium to be paid, when purchase orders have been accepted during the insurance period, while delivery takes place after expiry of the policy, i.e. does the pre-credit premium charge/surcharge adequately address this possibility. To help handle this, the insured would often be obliged to declare the delivery separately for the charge of premium, even if the policy has expired or been cancelled.

Some insurers follow the 'risk attaching system' with respect to orders accepted during the insurance period and resulting in delivery after expiry or cancellation of the policy. The same applies to the credit risk with respect to those orders: they remain insured. Other insurers, even those who follow the 'risk attaching system' for credit risks, cancel the pre-credit risk cover for the orders of non-delivered goods, as soon as the policy has expired or has been cancelled.

- ***Basis for the calculation of premium***

As indicated above, there are several conditions for declaration which (may) result in charging premium. Factors which may determine the premium rate or surcharge for pre-credit risk cover are the following:

- the length of the period of delivery

  This is the period between acceptance of the order and delivery of the goods. The longer this period, the higher the premium or surcharge. For some insurers this period starts at the acceptance of the order, because they cover the pre-credit risk with respect to the order. For other insurers this period starts from the first moment costs are made for this order.
- the type of goods

  Some insurers exclude goods which are not or not easily identifiable from pre-credit risk cover. Such goods can be commodities (e.g. vegetables and fruit), as well as goods with a highly volatile sales price such as crude oil, and gold. The same may apply to other highly perishable or fashionable goods.
- resale possibilities of the goods are of interest for the level of premium

  Goods delivered in packaging with the buyer's name or label are hard or impossible to resell elsewhere, when the buyer cannot or does not want to accept the goods.
- covered causes of loss

  In order to set the premium, it is important to know the type of insurance and which causes of loss are included: incidental cover or whole turnover insurance; discretionary limits or only limits set by the insurer; binding contracts/pending orders, insolvency, protracted default, political risk, consequential losses or liabilities (see also under Different types of pre-credit risk).

- ***Definition of protracted default before delivery***

The policy wording for protracted default before delivery should clarify:

- whether non-acceptance by the buyer as well as political risks preventing delivery to the buyer are insured
- the start of the claim filing/claim payment waiting period

***- Definition of covered costs***

The order accepted by the insured should lead to payment of the debt after delivery and in most cases a profitable transaction is intended. This means that the costs made for the order are lower than the amount of the debt/invoice to be paid. Profit is to be made after delivery and payment of the debt/invoice. Therefore profit is not normally indemnified in case of a claim payment for a pre-credit risk.

When the insured has incurred higher costs than the debt/invoice in case of delivery (a loss making transaction), most insurers limit the cover of these costs to the amount of the contract. A loss making transaction cannot be made profitable by claiming the high costs under pre-credit risk cover.

The costs incurred by the insured for the execution of an order have to be verifiable. Some insurers require that the costs for the execution concerning this order were made after a credit limit for the buyer has been applied for and established. This could imply that costs for spare parts or raw material purchased by the insured before the acceptance of the order and already in stock with him, are not to be included in the indemnification for pre-credit risk.

Insurers may avail themselves of experts to check the calculation of costs claimed by the insured as pre-credit risk.

***- Consequences of imminent loss or overdue accounts***

Not only might the cover of new credit risks be influenced by imminent losses or overdue accounts, but also the cover of new orders might be affected. Apart from the insured's obligation to notify the insurer and to ask for his intervention to collect outstanding debts, the insurer may have reason to give instructions to the insured. The insurer may also find reason to withdraw the credit limit which means end of cover for new orders.

- ***Consequences of the insurer's instructions***

In case the insurer wants to limit an imminent pre-credit risk loss, he needs knowhow and expertise of the trade sector concerned the goods under production, their resale possibilities, and the consequences of his instructions for the buyer, the insured and himself.

- ***Conflict of interests***

The parties involved in the pre-credit risk have different interests: the insured wants to complete a profitable transaction; the buyer wants to receive the goods it is entitled to; and the insurer wants to limit its losses. This may lead to a conflict of interests between two or more parties. The conditions for pre-credit risk cover should clarify the priority of the interests concerned.

- ***Losses in excess of the credit limit***

When setting a discretionary limit or applying for a credit limit set by the insurer, the insured should take into account the maximum outstanding balance and the amount of orders under production which did not yet result in delivery. But even when the credit limit is sufficient it may occur that the total pre-credit risk is in excess of the credit limit because of consequential losses or liabilities of the insured. In case these are to be covered, the setting or application of a higher credit limit could offer a solution.

- ***Allocation of recoveries***

Some insurers apply special conditions for the allocation of recoveries in case of pre-credit risk insurance. In case of a credit loss as well as a pre-credit loss the received recoveries are allocated with priority to the outstanding debts/invoices. A possible residual amount of recoveries will be allocated to the insured costs.

## ADVANTAGES FOR THE INSURED

The inclusion of pre-credit risk cover offers many advantages to the insured. It is an extension of cover which makes the policy more attractive as collateral, as when the policy claim indemnification has been assigned to a bank that has financed the insured's credit transactions.

Because the insurance cover starts earlier than delivery, there is an earlier signal of imminent losses. The insured as well as the insurer have a mutual obligation to be alert in case of a deterioration of the buyer's creditworthiness before delivery.

The premium rate is attractive, when compared to the premium the insured pays for the insurance of the credit risk. Usually, for the insurance of the pre-credit risk with a delivery period of, say, 3 months a percentage of the premium applicable for a credit term of 3 months is charged for the insurance of the pre-credit risk. Alternatively, sometimes a lump sum of additional premium is charged for pre-credit risk cover

By providing extended cover, there is a deeper involvement of the insurer with the risk.

## ADVANTAGES FOR THE INSURER

When insuring the pre-credit risk there is an earlier involvement of the insurer with the insured transaction, and more premium is received than under trade credit insurance only.

***Extra attention for:***

**- *Commencement of the pre-credit risk and the credit risk***

It should be clearly stipulated whether the pre-credit risk cover starts at the moment of acceptance of the order or when costs are made. Especially for the insurance of debts related to services it should be clear when the credit risk begins. For some insurers, the moment when the insured is entitled to payment from the buyer may be a factor. Partial invoices can also play a role. Other insurers let the credit risk start at the moment when all services enumerated in the order have been rendered or completed. The term of delivery in the policy should not be exceeded.

- ***Knowhow when giving instructions to the insured***

When the insurer gives instructions to the insured to limit possible loss, the insurer has to be aware of the consequences for all other parties involved in the transaction. In case the insurer lacks sufficient knowledge of the trade sector or of the goods to be delivered, it is usually necessary to employ an outside expert.

- ***Is the policy 'risk attaching' or 'losses occurring'?***

Because the commencement of the pre-credit risk is always earlier than the start of the credit risk, all consequences of the reduction or withdrawal of a credit limit and the expiry or cancellation of the policy are determined by the answer to the question whether a policy is 'risk attaching' or 'losses occurring'. In other words: does the policy cover risks which commenced during the insurance period or losses occurring during the insurance period?

This is also an important issue for the insured: was the order accepted the before commencement of the policy or was the transaction perhaps previously insured elsewhere? In the case of the latter, is it necessary to give retrospective cover for these orders or are they insured by the preceding insurer?

- ***Consequences of withdrawal of cover on a buyer or a country***

When the cover on a buyer or a country is withdrawn, this is mostly applicable for all credit limits established for that buyer or for all buyers in the country concerned. Some insurers get in touch with the insured that has a policy including pre-credit risk cover and ask whether there are orders in portfolio for these buyer(s). Subsequently the insurer will give instructions to reduce the risk. When insurers fail to give instructions, the insured faces a dilemma. Are they supposed to consider the withdrawal of the credit limit as adverse information and, ironically, should the insurer then be notified? This depends on the policy conditions.

- ***'Mixed' claims (partially pre-credit risk and partially credit risk)***
When a loss occurs or is imminent, it is important for the insurer to know if there are also outstanding debts related to deliveries at stake next to the accepted orders. Instructions to the insured will be determined by this outcome. Besides that, it is of interest to know how possible recoveries will be allocated.
In short:

- Pre-credit risk cover can be an important extension of the trade credit insurance cover. Extra knowhow is required, as well as extra attention and willingness to manage the risks.
- Pre-credit risk cover should not be recommended for every transaction of every insured, but where it does make sense, it may be of great value to the insured and profitable for the insurer.

CHAPTER 5

# Typical Set-up of a Trade Credit Insurance Contract

*The traditional whole turnover credit insurance contract typically takes the form of an umbrella policy, which contains a framework of terms and conditions under which individual amounts of cover (credit limits on the customer's buyers) are agreed during the lifetime of the policy.*

*The actual set-up and appearance may differ per credit insurer, but broadly speaking the credit insurance policy has the following parts and contents.*

## SCHEDULE

This contains details of the policyholder and of the individual policy, such as

- policy number;
- name and address of policyholder and of other parties to the policy (e.g. broker or trade financier);
- actual premium rate or amount and/or the minimum premium amount;
- start and end date of the policy (policy period);

- description of the insured's trade activities;
- covered percentage and amounts of deductibles, if any;
- the longest credit period that the insured may agree with its buyers under cover of the policy;
- the maximum amount that the insurer is liable to in respect of all losses during the policy period;
- specification of the costs that will be charged for credit limit handling and monitoring of the buyers;
- overview of buyer countries covered by the policy including any special terms and conditions for particular buyer countries;
- currency of the insurance contract;
- the applicable law and competent court.

## GENERAL TERMS AND CONDITIONS

This part contains generally applicable policy wording describing the insurer's commitment, what is covered and what not and the rules of conduct, duties and obligations of the policyholder required for coverage. It covers subject such as:

- description of the covered causes of loss (insolvency, protracted default, political risks);
- description of the insured receivables or trade;
- exclusions (which causes of loss, which buyers, which receivables are not covered);
- when cover for each receivable starts (typically for credit risk cover, when the corresponding delivery is made or when the service is performed);
- credit limits: how and when to apply or establish for a credit limit for each buyer, how long are they valid, any discretionary limits that may be set by the policyholders themselves, the right of the credit insurers to change credit limit amount;
- what the policyholder should do to avoid or minimise a potential loss, such as take active collection measures, report

non-paying buyers to the insurer, hand over the collection to a specialist collection agency);

- claims handling: when can the policyholder submit a claim, how is the insured loss and indemnification calculated, how are deductibles applies, how are payments from the buyer or proceeds allocated;
- premium and declaration: what and when should the policyholder declare for premium calculation (for example, the total amount of sales in the past month or the total outstanding balances at the end of each month);
- how will premium be charged (e.g. in arrears, in advance, fixed premium per policy period) and any premium bonus/surcharge arrangement that may apply to the policy;
- general obligations of the policyholder, such as disclosure of facts relevant or the insured risk, consequences of non-observance of the policy obligations;
- miscellaneous: confidentiality clause, data protection clauses, transfer of policy rights, currency conversion rules and exchange rate, how and when the policy will be renewed or may be cancelled.

## ADDITIONAL OR CUSTOMER SPECIFIC CONDITIONS, CLAUSES, MODULES

Next to the Schedule and the General Conditions, policies may contain additional clauses, modules or endorsements that customise the policy to the specific needs or trading practices or procedures of the individual policyholder or that capture the idiosyncrasies of the trade sector (like the building and construction sector or transport sector).

CHAPTER 6

# Premium: The Price for Cover

*Before the prospect decides to accept the proposed conditions for cover, negotiations may focus on several aspects of a policy: general provisions, credit limits, specific conditions and, of course, the premium rate. Every insurer has proprietary pricing tools to calculate a premium rate but some of the common pricing building blocks are mentioned in this chapter.*

When a prospect applies for a credit insurance policy, the insurer knows which parameters to take into account for the premium rate he will offer.

- ***The subjective risk***

The prospect gives details of its company and trade sector, the usual credit terms agreed upon, credit management procedures, the current outstanding receivables and the losses sustained in the past. The insurer can check the creditworthiness of the prospect and may decide whether to start a business relation or decline to make any offer. When the prospect is a member of a trade sector association and maintains a credit management policy aimed at the prevention of losses, this may be a reason for the insurer to include a premium discount in the calculation of the premium rate.

- ***The objective risk***

Details about the portfolio of buyers will determine the premium rate to a great extent. The following elements may play a role:

- the volume of turnover;
- the spread of risks;
- the trade sector of the buyers;
- the creditworthiness of the buyers;
- the possible inclusion of cover of political risks;
- the buyers' domicile(s) and respective sovereign creditworthiness;
- the possible inclusion of the pre-credit risk and the average/maximum delivery period;
- a monthly declaration of whole turnover or of outstanding receivables
- the credit term agreed upon with the buyers;
- the effective credit term;
- the loss history;
- the percentage of cover applied for;
- the possible inclusion of a bonus/malus arrangement;
- the inclusion of deductibles such as a non-qualifying loss, an each and every first loss, a threshold or an aggregate first loss.

- ***The insurer***

- experience, and development of results;
- the price and the conditions of reinsurance;
- overall claims ratio and cost ratio;
- the aimed profit margin;
- the creativity, competence and commercial approach of the policy underwriter.

- ***The country of the insurer***

- the legal measures which have influence on the pricing of a policy (taxes, subsidies, conditions for the liquidity of insurers);
- the market situation (is it a buyers' or a sellers' market?) and the competition between insurers.

- ***The broker/agent/sales person (as applicable)***
  - the creativity of the distribution channel and its influence and commercial approach.

The best way for a prospect to find out what the price of the policy will be is a direct question to a broker or a credit insurer. Rarely will the insurer's annual report give an answer to the question what its average premium has been in the past: Comparing the insured turnover and the aggregate premium income will not result in an adequate answer for any specific case, because the above mentioned parameters may lead to a completely different outcome.

## HOW TO CHARGE PREMIUM

Since there is a relation between the premium rate and the objective risk, there are different ways to charge the premium on details of the insured turnover.

Many insurers calculate the amount of premium to be paid by multiplying the premium rate and the amount of the insured turnover. Monthly, quarterly or annual declarations of the insured turnover may lead to premium invoices.

Other insurers may require monthly declarations of the insured amounts outstanding and charge these amounts with the premium rate.

Specific premium rates may be related to certain countries, groups of countries or payment conditions agreed upon with the buyer and specified in the policy. This requires detailed and specific declarations of whole turnover of outstanding amounts.

Some insurers have a system to charge premium on the total amounts of credit limits issued under a policy.

The expected premium to be paid in one insurance year may be divided into monthly or quarterly instalments to be invoiced in order to maintain the insurer's cash flow.

Related to the expected premium the insurer may charge a minimum premium to be paid per annum.

A bonus/malus arrangement in the policy may lead to a rebate of premium or an additional charge of premium depending on the claims ratio. The amount of minimum premium to be paid may overrule the consequences of a rebate of premium.

Finally there are policies where no declaration of whole turnover or outstanding amounts is to be made, but where a fixed annual amount is charged.

CHAPTER 7

# Day-to-Day Policy Management

*Companies invest in trade credit insurance for a variety of reasons, including:*

- *Sales expansion – If receivables are insured, a company can safely sell more to existing buyers, or go after new buyers that may have been felt to be too risky without insurance.*
- *Expansion into new international markets.*
- *Better financing terms – In many cases a bank will lend more capital against insured receivables and may also reduce the cost of funds.*
- *Reduce bad-debt reserves – This frees up cash for the company. Also, trade credit insurance premiums are tax deductible, but bad debt reserves are not.*
- *Indemnification from buyer non-payment.*

The process of insuring accounts receivable involves understanding a company's trade sector, risk philosophy, business strategy, financial health, funding requirements and internal credit management expertise. The ultimate goal is not only indemnify losses incurred from a trade debt default but also to help the insured avoid catastrophic losses and grow their business profitably. The key is having the right information to make informed credit decisions and therefore avoid or minimize losses.

A trade credit insurance policy does not replace a company's credit practices, but rather supplements and enhances the job of a credit professional. The best credit insurers will invest heavily in the development of proprietary credit and financial information, and also will employ risk analysts, as well as industry- and country-based underwriters, in many geographic locations in order to have a close physical presence to its customers' buyers. The better credit insurers will also analyse payment information about the insured buyers to identify early signs of financial trouble.

At the start of negotiations the would-be insured describes the risk structure of the business it wants to insure in a document known as the application form. This contains all the details on the insured's own business and about its buyers that are required for assessing the risk profile. The details on the insured itself serve not only to categorise the company in terms of sector, products, market standing etc. but also assess the subjective risk, aspects such as professionalism, management quality and mentality and solvency. The other side of the story is the risk profile of the buyer portfolio. To assess these details are needed on the potential buyers, such as their names, locations/domiciles, numbers, size, turnovers and outstanding receivables, terms of payment and payment periods, payment history, defaults, etc.

An advance review of the buyers is often carried out to gain an impression of the financial standing of the buyer portfolio. Comparing the actual credit limits with the limits applied-for yields the acceptance rate. The risk profile thus obtained for the business to be insured serves as the basis for agreeing on the terms and conditions of the policy so as to achieve the best possible match for both parties. It is also the basis for calculating and quoting the premium. The premium is usually expressed as a percentage of the insured monthly turnover or of the balances open at the end of the month. In exceptional cases the insured may also be offered a fixed premium, i.e. a pre-defined premium per year regardless of turnover. If applicable and/or pursuant to local regulations, the annual creditworthiness-review fees plus turnover tax/VAT (Value Added Tax) per credit limit and any insurance premium tax are paid in addition to the insurance premium.

Having successfully negotiated and agreed on terms and conditions of a trade credit insurance policy for a certain insurance period, the quality of the insurer's policy management and his customer service are decisive for the insured's satisfaction and willingness at the end of the insurance period to renew the policy or extend the insurance period. The job of the insurer's account manager who is the day-to-day contact for the insured and/or broker starts taking care of the following issues to establish the policy and make it workable for both parties:

- the policy has to be physically issued by the insurer, sent to the insured and/or broker, countersigned and returned (one copy) to the insurer;
- all credit limits promised during the negotiation phase have to be properly issued on credit limit documents;
- operational staff of the insured have to be well informed on policy rules and trained in policy handling for enabling them to fulfil the obligations of the insured (among them: when and how to communicate with the insurer for new credit limit applications, for turnover or outstanding balance declarations, for non-payment notifications and claims notifications);
- access to the online system of the insurer (if there is any) has to be made technically available for the operational staff of the insured.

Differently from other insurance lines, the trade credit insurance policy has to be continuously managed by the insurer after the policy-establishing phase described above because the policy is made to cover payment default risks of the insured's future business – and the development and structure of that business during the insurance period is not 100% predictable. It may be at any day that:

- the insured wants to sell its products to new buyers in countries that have not been included into the list of covered countries in the policy;
- longer or different credit terms than agreed in the policy are requested by the insured's buyers for specific reasons (sometimes only seasonally);
- new business lines or products are to be launched by the insured that were not expected when policy terms had been calculated and negotiated and therefore not covered by the policy;
- the insured finds out that credit risks which he initially had not judged as relevant enough to be insured (e.g. pre-credit risks) became more important and should be covered by the policy.

In such cases the account manager will elaborate and suggest solutions how to adapt the policy to the extended needs of the insured at appropriate terms.

The account manager's aim is to build and maintain a good and trustful customer relationship. They are the insured's main contact if and when the insured is dissatisfied with a decision or communication from any department of the insurer (for instance from credit limit underwriting, from claims handling or from premium invoicing). The account manager investigates what has happened on the insurer's and insured's side, if any misunderstanding or mistake or misleading communication has triggered the conflict, and then takes action to solve it. The more the account manager delivers solutions or offers compromises acceptable for both parties the more he gains trust from the insured and the more he tightens the relationship. Invitations to seminars, to workshops or to other events organised by the insurer are further actions of the account manager for strengthening the customer relationship.

It is obvious that also the broker (or agent for certain markets) can play a role in the day-to-day policy management, by advising the insured and supporting his compliance with the conditions of the policy.

# COMPLIANCE TO POLICY OBLIGATIONS REGARDING LOSS MINIMIZATION

In order to visualise the procedure of credit management related to the credit insurance policy a time table may be helpful to the insured, who wants to comply with the obligations of the policy.

The timetable is meant to be an example. The specific conditions of a policy will clarify the terms to be complied with and the consequences of exceeding the terms for notification and requests for intervention.

**Timetable**

Example:
-Credit term: 30 days after date of invoice
-Maximum credit term: 60 days after date of invoice

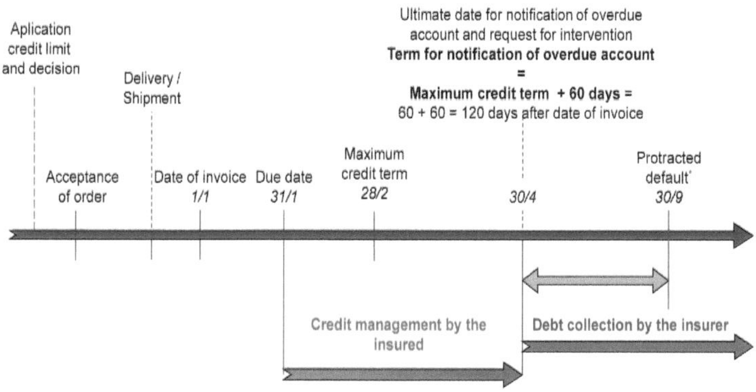


- Indemnification is paid within 1 month after insolvency or in case of protracted default 6 months after due date or by other insurers 5 months after notification of overdue account and request for intervention.

When the policy includes pre-credit cover the timetable should start at the moment of accepting the order from the buyer. Between that date and the delivery or shipment of the goods or the completion of services a manufacturing or delivery period should not exceed the maxim term mentioned in the policy.

From delivery or shipment of the goods or the completion of services the credit term starts, which should not exceed the maximum credit term mentioned in the policy. Some insurers allow an extension of the originally agreed credit term as long as the maximum credit term is respected by the insured.

On the due date of the invoice the buyer is obliged to pay. If the buyer does not pay precisely by the due date, the policy may nevertheless include a period of time starting from due date and during which new deliveries or shipments may still be covered, but following which new deliveries or shipments would not be covered. Also, during this period, the insured may not be required to report the buyer as technically overdue.

After expiry of that period, a notification of an overdue account should normally be sent to the insurer. Some insurers require that the insured sends a request for intervention at the same date, others allow for an extra period.

When the insured fears an imminent loss even before the expiry of the period for notification and request for intervention, he may notify the insurer earlier in order to minimize the risk.

CHAPTER 8

# Buyer Risk Underwriting in Trade Credit Insurance

*One of the important aspects of trade credit insurance is the credit assessment that is duly made in respect of all buyers in an insured's portfolio.*

*This credit assessment is used to determine the level of coverage for each of the insured's buyers in case of loss. Furthermore, it is a tool that helps to avoid potential defaults, bearing in mind that the insurer controls the financial and economic situation of each buyer throughout the validity of the policy, duly assessing any new information becoming available and effectively acting as a true credit control department.*

*The following is a detailed description of the working methods normally used by insureds in order to manage their risk by means of a credit insurance policy. It also describes the main tasks implemented by risk underwriting teams from an insurer's perspective.*

## THE INSURED'S PERSPECTIVE

Whenever an insured has signed a credit insurance policy, in keeping with the provisions of the policy, he shall provide the insurer with a full list of buyers to whom he sells on credit. The list initially submitted should include the following information:

- details of each buyer (company name, VAT number or registered company number, address and country);
- amount of the credit limit required for each buyer;
- means of payment to be used by each buyer and any securities such as guarantees that may already be in place;
- the insured may include any further information or observations they consider convenient for the insurer's risk anlaysis team.

On the basis of the information provided, the insurer then establishes credit limits for each buyer and may grant full, partial or no coverage whatsoever in respect of the requested credit limits. In the case of a qualified decision (i.e. involving limitations or exclusions), an insurer will usually indicate the grounds for such decision being made.

At this point, the full portfolio of buyers will have been duly rated and for as long as the policy is in force, insured may request credit limits for new buyers or apply for modifications of previously established (or formerly excluded) credit limits.

Likewise, during the policy term, unless the limit has been issued on a non-cancelable basis, the insurer may modify any credit limits previously granted. Accordingly, constant monitoring of the full buyer portfolio by the insurer may lead to new information being obtained that would make it convenient to qualify or change its initial decision.

Most insurers have an online system to enable insureds to manage their credit insurance policies and particularly, all credit limits established thereunder. These tools allow insureds to process requests for credit ratings and even to obtain automatic replies. Furthermore, these online systems ensure that any credit limits granted are easily integrated into the insured's own IT systems whenever required.

As well as providing access to full information on credit limits, insurers usually provide contact details of the person(s) in the risk underwriting team who may be contacted for further information or clarification of credit limits.

Thus, insurers may go beyond merely compensating an insured for any loss incurred in case of default (which is a strictly insurance-related function) and in some cases become a form of extended credit control department that monitors the insured's clients. Accordingly, this ensures that for each credit limit granted, a detailed economic and financial analysis has been carried out to determine the probability of each buyer defaulting on payment.

## RISK UNDERWRITING PROCESS: AN INSURER'S PERSPECTIVE

The risk underwriting process in credit insurance has advanced significantly in recent years, in both technical and technological terms.

From a technical point of view, credit risk management techniques have undergone a fundamental change applying actuarial and statistical methods. The majority of insurers have been able to develop sophisticated statistical models to calculate the Probability of Default (PD) for each buyer. The PD is translated into a rating reflecting the credit quality of each buyer. The rating is the basis for the final decision in respect of any credit limits to be established.

These statistical models were developed as a result of the data accumulated by insurers from their experience with default and the fact that it had become possible to store (in processable, structured formats) the appropriate data with the required quality and time span.

Although it is difficult to generalise, insurers are nonetheless able to develop different types of algorithms for separate business segments (large, medium and small enterprises) or for different industries or even for different countries, since the predictive capacity of the data may vary significantly, depending on the group in question.

Accordingly, the statistical models created by each insurer will take very diverse data into account and although economic-financial ratios are extremely important in terms of weight and predictability, they are not the only elements to be taken into consideration and can be used in combination with other more qualitative data.

The technical aspects of credit insurance have evolved rapidly; nonetheless, these statistical models would be of little use without analysts or underwriters who are familiar with them and are capable of interpreting them correctly and able to enhance them with qualitative assessments or correct any weaknesses therein, if necessary. Accordingly insurers allocate a great deal of their resources to experts specializing in risk underwriting.

Credit insurance underwriting has also advanced significantly in terms of technology, which has made it much simpler to create the aforementioned statistical models, bringing greater responsiveness and efficiency to the whole decision-making process.

The different technological advances have meant an increasingly greater volume of data and, at the same time, better data accessibility and processability. To a greater or lesser extent, all insurers have been able to work with data providers to create sophisticated technological systems for data collection, integration and processing that facilitate efficient management of their risk portfolio (comprising millions of companies). For example, the information that might be processed by an insurer in its data base could include:

***a) Information from external sources:***

- details of each buyer (including information relating to the business activity (age of the company, number of employees, branch offices), markets in which he operates, shareholders and affiliates, management team, etc.);
- complete financial data: annual accounts, annual report, audit report;
- commercial registry data: date of incorporation, modifications of share capital and shareholders, takeovers, mergers, winding-up, etc.;

- information from bad buyer registers (via credit bureau);
- information relating to any legal proceedings;
- daily media releases; on a specific buyer, line of business, country.

***b) Information from internal sources:***

- information referring to any payment-related incidents, e.g. requested extensions of payment;
- information relating to losses/claims from all insured;
- reports made by analysts followings visits to buyers.

Correct management of this huge amount of information will be a key factor in determining credit limits and ultimately, in providing the best possible service to the insured. In this sense, credit insurance is deeply embedded and involved in the business activities of insured, which means that credit insurers have to be agile in their decisions. Accordingly, in the vast majority of cases, they respond to a request for a credit limit to be established in less than 24 hours of receipt of the insured's application.

In the following pages the risk underwriting process is comprehensively described.

## STANDARD REQUIREMENTS

Credit limits may be assessed based either on quantity data, such as financial statements, or on quality elements. Assessing a credit limit is more objective when financial statements are available. Nevertheless, being the publication of balance sheets non-mandatory in most countries, the gathering of unofficial financial data through information sources may be hard. All this makes it necessary to take other quality elements into consideration, helping the underwriter to work out a credit limit proposal. Within the assessment process, official data must be reviewed separately from unofficial data. Every information package must contain the following elements:

Public data: chamber of commerce registration, stock capital, incorporation details, company name, management composition, balance-sheet information plus any arrangement with creditors, legal proceedings or protests. If the buyer belongs to a group, data gathering must include the whole group structure, the holding company and the components of the board of directors.

Non-public data: number of employees, market position, major insured, major buyers, location and size of offices, age and experience of exponents, exponents' personal wealth, experience of insured and banks, payment scoring, judgement and assessment by the information sources.

***Risk assessment***

Risk assessment must include the following procedural steps, according to whether financial information is available or not.

***When financial data are available:***

- conformity check between the buyer company name in the request and the buyer company name in the information report. The credit limit decision must always be related to the official company name, as reported in the chamber of commerce certificate and specified by the source;
- reclassification of financial statements including footnotes, when complete;
- preparation of the scoring model;
- assessment of the information report;
- assessment of the prospect or the insured (in case of policy already issued), including size, percentage of exported turnover, minimum supply;
- policy structure in terms of loss ratio records, deductibles etc.;
- country assessment;
- financial statements along with auditor's report and the according notes (may give answers to open questions as listed in the sections that follow further down).

***When financial data are not available:***

- conformity check between the buyer company name in the request and the buyer company name in the information report. The credit limit decision must always be related to the official company name, as reported in the chamber of commerce certificate and specified by the source;
- assessment of the information report, with special reference to
- years of business;
- principals' age and experience;
- payment trend;
- experience of banks and insured;
- location and size of offices;
- market position;
- major insured and buyers;
- connections with other companies;
- information source's opinion;
- exporter's assessment;
- country assessment.

## THE RISK UNDERWRITING DEPARTMENT SHOULD BE AWARE THAT:

- an assessment of the policyholder and the type of policy must also be taken into account
- financial data become outdated and should be refreshed: in the best case every 3–6 months; but no later than 2–3 years.

***Sensitive risks***

'Sensitive risks' are those buyers meeting the following conditions:

- incorporation and/or business starting date < 1 year from analysis, unless the company has a prior working experience under a different name;

- payment difficulties (irregular payments, protests, indemnifications);
- unfavourable financial situation/negative net equity;
- arrangements with creditors/insolvency;
- shareholders' bad records;
- connections with companies in crisis;
- buyer located in high risk country.

In addition, the risk underwriting department must also assess whether there is high concentration of credit limit requests in a short time period (as this might point to a higher risk of fraud).

***Risk monitoring***

For the risk prevention and monitoring process to be correct, the current exposure on each buyer must be periodically checked. A check of current credit limits must be made on the basis of an updated information report and with the help of IT system alerts that warn the underwriter of any risk situation. As a result, the following services should be set up:

- a permanent 'watch' service, if possible, from the information sources, warning of any unfavourable situations during the waiting year;
- a yearly information report renewal service;
- qualitative information exchange with other departments (claims, recovery, portfolio, etc.);
- a check of market and trade trends;
- a check of the political and economic development of the country.

***The tools and functions that help and support risk assessment***

The following will help improve the buyer/insured evaluation process and the monitoring of exposures, in order to keep the insurer's loss ratio in check:

- External information sources: It is advisable to consult several sources on every insured country so that the information collected is more likely to be certain. If possible, information providers must be local and the insurer's internal officer in charge of information sources should meet with the providers at least once a year, in order to monitor the service quality and processing times carefully.

- Proprietary management information: there are several statistics which can be used in support of risk assessment, the most indispensable of which may be the loss ratio, which can be analysed per policy, country, trade sector, etc.

## ANALYSING THE RISK

The following guidelines may apply for insurers:

1) Assess the buyer/insured in terms of an objective maximum credit limit and maximum liability, without being conditioned by the amount of the request.
2) Reconcile the need for rapid decision with the requirement for deeper analysis.
3) Check 'internal' information such as exposures, list of losses/extensions, technical trend, records of credit limits, whether the buyer is also an insured, etc.
4) Generally speaking, analysing one fiscal year may not be sufficient for the granting of a credit limit. The whole buyer company trend should be reviewed by comparing the financial statements of different fiscal years.
5) Whenever the buyer company is a member of a group or a subsidiary to a holding company or has significant connections with other companies, the analysis should be extended to the holding company and the affiliated companies.
6) Use more care for those buyers that work in especially risky trade sectors.
7) Using the web, check whether the buyer appears on any international Black List, whenever the country, type of business and/or collected information make this doubt arise.
8) Store in the IT system any information that may be useful for the future.

For the credit risk underwriting department:

1) So that all companies in a similar trade sector can compete equally, it is reasonable to grant the same level of buyer coverage in cases where similar amounts of credit limit are being requested by different policyholders (assuming the insurer has available capacity);
2) Extra care should be given to decisions related to perishable supplies;
3) Check that the buyer's business is consistent with the applicant policyholder's business;
4) Assess the damage that may result from credit limit cancellation, termination or withdrawal (see sensitive risks).

## ANALYSIS OF THE BUYERS: GENERAL ASSESSMENT

The following guidelines may apply:

1. Assess the buyer's competitive position in its industry, taking into consideration competitors' trends.
2. Pay attention to any unfavourable information (protests, defaults, mortgages, injunctions to pay, seizures) or bad payment records and/or reserves against the buyer.
3. Keep a cautionary behaviour whenever the following occurs in seeking trade information:

- difficult identification of properties;
- recent and/or numerous changes of ownership;
- recent and/or numerous changes of managers or directors;
- young age of exponents;
- significant age difference among exponents lacking any family relationships;
- recent and/or numerous changes of company names;
- recent and/or numerous changes of address;
- recent and/or numerous changes of company purpose;
- capital stock reduction following bad financial investments or improper extra-company behaviours;

- excessive number of requests, either directly to you or to the information source;
- inconsistency between the buyer's business and the reference sector's business;
- impossible collection of significant receivables (domino effect);
- new important competitors entering the market;
- banks are withdrawing credit lines or requesting collateral guarantees before extending existing credit lines.

4. Review the policyholder's capability for risk undertaking (this may be deduced from the loss trend of policy or direct knowledge of the insured).
5. Take any worsening of the rating suggested by the information sources into due consideration.
6. Assess the consistency of key ratios, namely the Equity to Debt ratio and the coverage of Fixed Assets, especially where Net Equity is negative.
7. Assess the item 'Personnel Cost' in comparison with the number of employees reported by the information source.
8. Compare the amount of Accounts receivable and Stocks with other balance-sheet items, especially Sales. In this framework, check the trend of turnover indicators (buyers, inventories, working capital).
9. Analyse how the economic result is obtained based on: Added Value, Gross Operating Margin (EBITDA, Earnings before interest, taxes, depreciation and amortization), Operating Result (EBIT, Earnings before interest and tax), ROS (Return on sales) and ROI (Return on investment).
10. After an acceptable depreciation level, the EBIT should be positive. A favourable element may be the use of accelerated and/or anticipated depreciation or the presence of non-deductible allocations. Thus an analysis of the item 'Taxes and duties' is needed.
11. Pay special attention to the balancing of short-term maturities, by comparing the items 'Current assets' with 'Current liabilities'.

12. Examine the major balance-sheet indicators and assess their trend over the years.
13. Consider the 'Extraordinary items' with special care. Bad results are often hidden behind 'Extraordinary costs'. Lacking any information, check that extraordinary gains are non-recurrent and extraordinary losses are not repeatable.
14. It is recommendable to compare the trend of all balance-sheet items over the years
15. Pay attention to the comments contained in footnotes.

For the credit risk underwriting department, fraud can be prevented by asking the following information to the policyholder itself:

- What is the buyer's real address?
- What is the buyer's behaviour on price elasticity?
- Has the buyer offered guarantees from unknown guarantors?
- How the buyer was contacted and how old are the relations with the policyholder? In which period of the year was the contact established? Consider that the days before Christmas or tourist seasons are most exposed to fraud risk.
- Has the buyer urged the policyholder to use credit insurance?
- Has the policyholder asked visited the buyer at its premises?

## ANALYSIS OF COMPANIES: ADVANCED FINANCIAL ANALYSIS

In addition to the above, other elements of analysis may be needed:

***General:***

- If the company is publicly listed, the trends of stock and bond prices as well as Credit Default Swap spreads are important indicators of how the market is responding to the company. Significant changes of the value of stock prices should be considered as a warning sign. Likewise, an unexpected volume of negotiations on a listed company may indicate undisclosed news;

- Pay attention to Memorandum Accounts and make a careful reading of the Additional Remarks and Management Report. In particular, watch out for the effect of derivative contracts;
- If financial statements are not certified or auditors change frequently or sizeable payments are made to auditors without a reason, all this may arouse suspicion.

## FINANCIAL STATEMENTS/FIXED ASSETS:

***Definition of fixed assets:***
Goods not for sale which remain useful for the company over several years.

These are divided into:

- *Non-operational assets:* farming lands, town buildings, building areas, etc. whose uses are separated and independent of the corporate business. If assets are purchased based on a preliminary contract, the residual amount to be paid will be shown in the liabilities.
- *Operational assets:* their property value is needed to understand the extent of the company's equity and their economic value is needed to understand how they influence the making of results. This is useful to measure how much rigour has been applied to the preparation of the financial statements and what the actual profitability of the company may be.
- Operational assets include industrial buildings, buildings and lands used for the company's core business, including offices and personnel housings:
- *plants that cannot be removed*;
- *plants that can be removed*: the machinery which can be removed and used somewhere else keeping their value fully or almost fully intact. In addition to the above elements, we basically need to know the typical quantity indicators (e.g. daily grinding capacity, number of fuses, etc.) of these plants;

- *vehicle fleet*: these should be noted only if significant and used for the transport of goods outside the company (thus excluding personal cars of company owners); depending on their quantity, a query at the Public Register for Automobiles or Ship Register or Railway Authority may be needed. Their preservation status is especially important;
- *furniture and fittings*: office, warehouse or shop furniture and equipment are to be assessed only if significant;
- *intangible goods*: property or exclusive patents, licenses and concessions. If their value is significant, we need to know the nature, expiration, degree of exploitation, any privileges to third parties and in particular the advantage for the company;
- *depreciable costs*: start-up costs and expenses for incorporation, goodwill, Research and Development, discounts for the issue of debenture loans, etc.;
- *fixed assets in the course of construction*: payments for plants or installations under construction. We need to know the nature and expected amount of any future costs;
- *depreciation provisions*: the total amount of operational assets must be deducted from the accounts where allocations are recorded – usually in the liabilities – including details. Out of these, we need to know the absolute and percentage increase compared to the value of the corresponding assets and the adjustment, if any, of depreciation rates.

***Financial:***

Shareholdings: the term Shareholdings means durable investments in other businesses, usually in the form of company shares or stakes. Capital contributions need to be identified, namely the shares in other companies having a common interest, and the type of relationship (subsidiaries, affiliates, holding company) as well as the percentage of investment. Record any signature commitments taken by the insured for its affiliates. If the item Shareholding is significant, it is necessary to know how shares are valued, e.g. at purchasing cost or net equity cost, etc., whether these companies are listed or certified, whether this item may conceal potential losses and to what extent.

***Receivables:***

- *from affiliates*, including those originating from actual trade transactions of a given importance;
- *from partners or shareholders for capital contributions*, except if calls for payment or capital increase are at a very short term and these receivables can be considered as 'working capital';
- *from private individuals, non-affiliated companies with or without an interest*. We need to know the name of buyers, acceptance date, refund term, interest rate and guarantees;
- *investments for income*, retention, welfare or other reasons such as precious metals, unlisted market securities or other. If given for guarantee, they can be considered as 'working capital'.

Other securities: the term security means government-backed bonds or bonds issued by public entities and companies. It is necessary to see whether these are listed or not and if they can imply potential value or income losses.

***Commercial:***

Assets that, although referring to commercial transactions, cannot be collected within 12 months, are:

- *slow moving stocks*: unsold stocks or dead inventories; this figure could be deduced from the extent of goods included in the working capital;
- *bad, frozen or stagnating debts* whose collection date is not defined and/or the extent of realization is uncertain, unless it is decided to wholly remove them from the 'receivables';
- *bonds*: valuables of any kind (cash, securities, commodities, etc.) held by third parties as caution money, either for provisional or final use, either coming from the company's wealth or from third party's means.

***Deeper analysis***

- What is the actual value of intangible fixed assets? Is it guaranteed or may it be subject to strong devaluation if the company goes bankrupt? It is reminded that highly prudential assessment methods imply, for example, the removal of goodwill from equity, if the company does not produce income for several fiscal years.
- It is worrying to notice that the gains from the sale of plants and machinery that are useful for production are often used to generate cash/support daily cash transactions. Moreover, have they been written up with respect to their historical cost? Are plants and machinery sufficient to support production, besides being technologically advanced and environmentally friendly?

## SHORT-TERM ASSETS

***Definition of Working Capital or current and liquid assets***

This item includes the assets which are expected to rotate during the standard course of business in maximum 12 months from the balance-sheet or interim report date.

***Stock:***

- *consumer materials*: ancillary goods flowing into the construction of commodities;
- *raw materials: which are the basic supply for the company's production;*
- *work in progress*: a subdivision used by large companies, whose work is also or mainly made on commission, using long production cycles;
- *finished products* or finished product stocks for purely trade companies;
- *advances to insured*: a distinction should be made of balances and down payments and of standard procurement and coverage of sales contracts. There is a need for a list of

payments by kind and quantity, divided into goods stocked at company warehouse or at third party's warehouse for working, sale or guarantee purposes. What is the valuation criterion (purchasing, market or selling price)? What is the assessment method? When summarizing the company's financial and economic situation, any potential differences stemming from a prudential assessment of current market prices can be reckoned in the 'Internal reserves'. On the same occasion, it is good to check the use of any 'Provision for stock fluctuations' under the liabilities. While assessing the value of commodities, it is good to ask the client and/or calculate ourselves the stock turnover rate, because any decrease or increase compared to past rates may imply a difficulty in procurement or sale, respectively.

***Trade and other receivables:***

These refer to goods sold and still unpaid, whose payment is expected in 12 months:

- *from buyers*: receivables vs. agents or dealers who have acted as buyers on their own behalf;
- *portfolio*: sales against direct payment, IOU's (I Owe You's), drafts, goods documentary evidence – either in cash or deposited in banks after collection – received from or drawn on clients or issued against sales. It is necessary to identify the drafts expiring after 12 months to include them among the 'commercial fixed assets'.

***Cash:***

Money or easily convertible equivalents:

- *large-market listed securities* (restricted market securities are to be considered as 'Financial fixed assets'): we need to know the recording method (cost value or market value, whichever is lower), to understand whether significant losses are likely to occur;

- *banks*: available money in euros, with the exclusion of the collections under the item 'Receivables', and in foreign currency;
- *cash on hand*;
- *existing bank lines*; liquidity secured (special caution on this in case short-term liquidity is strained; quick-ratio).

***Prepaid expenses and accrued income:***
The income accrued and not yet collected and the expenses prepaid but not yet accrued (e.g. interests from payment extension and early collection of rentals): usually these do not deserve special investigation.

***Deeper analysis***
- Check whether the investments shown are negotiable and how easily they may be liquidated. Another important analysis is whether they are subject to any real guarantee.
- Check that net receivables are fully collectable and the allocations to the adjustment provision are correct without dangerous influences of tax laws. Another good rule is to examine buyer portfolio in terms of geographical location or to assess dangerous risk concentrations.

## SHORT-TERM LIABILITIES

***Financial:***
Money subsidies, including the following payables:
- *short term bank liabilities*: all types of bank guarantees and bank loans and overdrafts;
- *financial payables* of any kind according to the following list including the instalments whose expiry date is unfixed or unfixable, or it is expected within 12 months;
- *loans*, bonds, forward borrowings, consolidated debts including instalments expiring in 12 months;

- *from silent partners* (or shareholders): payables to limited partners however originated;
- *from affiliated companies*;
- *from private individuals*, family people, company administrators or employees. The more expensive is the cost of money, the more these types of financing are looked for.

***Commercial and various:***
commitments corresponding to the price of purchased goods or the amount of accrued liabilities (fees, wages, salaries, tax charges, commissions to agents, paid rentals, etc.). Their existence is certain because, although a company is not seeking for commercial or financial credit, purchasing or cost accrual time is not always simultaneous with actual payment time. Including the following payables:

- *from insured*: these are buyers for which the company owns accepted drafts or promissory notes, all of them expiring in 12 months. Supplies with extended payment terms based on agreements with creditors are to be included in 'deferred payables';
- *buyer advance payments*: we need to know the amount of the advance compared to the amount of the supply or service, whether a price revision is included – this is a long-cycle production – and whether the buyer can meet the agreed conditions, subject to penalties;
- *for taxes and duties*;
- *for salaries*, wages and social-security contributions. We need to know whether the company is compliant with payment terms, or has requested extensions or division into instalments;
- *various*: dividends in arrears, commissions to dealers or agents, payables to group companies for purchases at arm's-length terms, which may be considered as trade payables.

***Deeper analysis:***

- Analysis of loans per type. Are they being used or can they be suspended on demand? Based on the terms and conditions of their issue, we can understand how the banking system treats the company.
- What part of financial investments is to be refunded in a short-time period?

***Deferred or medium/long-term liabilities:***

Based on special agreements, the expiration of these liabilities is longer than 12 months from the balance-sheet date. Or their expiry date is not defined, but one can be sure that they will not be paid before 12 months. Including the following payables:

- *mortgage loans*, debenture bonds and forward borrowings, including the instalments expiring in the subsequent 12 months. We need to know: the loan opening date, the loan purpose, the lending people – especially if shareholders – or entities, any division into instalments, depreciation schemes, final repayment dates, renewals, if any, any right for early termination, the interest rate, any guarantees (real-estate mortgages; privileges on machinery, plants, concessions, patents, etc.; personal guarantees), bank or insurance guarantees;
- *consolidated payables to silent partners* or shareholders: company payables to unlimited partners (receivables against unlimited partners are recorded as 'equity') having a characteristic of stability;
- *to group companies* (subsidiaries or affiliates);
- *to private individuals*, family people, company administrators, managers or employees as described above.

The following payables are also included:

- *taxes and duties*;
- *personnel severance pays*: the money due to personnel leaving the company under the law or the contract.

It is necessary to know whether balance-sheet entries are updated and sufficient, in arithmetic terms, to cover the whole company liability or they are inadequate.

***Provisions:***

Prudential allocations to cover future losses or expected or likely expenses, whose extent or date of occurrence are not certain.

These may include:

- commodity price fluctuations;
- bad debts;
- plant maintenance and repair costs: these are needed to compare their percentage against the corresponding asset items;
- taxes and duties;
- various provisions: fluctuations of securities and exchange rates, claims, non-insured risks, etc.

***Accrued expenses and deferred income:***

The expenses accrued and not yet paid and the income collected but not yet accrued: usually these do not deserve special investigation.

***Profits:***

Divided into:

- profits from past fiscal years and profits from the current year arising from the 'P&L account';
- profits to be distributed, if made by family enterprises or however to be reinvested in the company.

***Equity:***

This is the company's wealth (and available towards third-party creditors if the need arose).

According to the type of company:

- one-man companies: net surplus;
- unregistered companies: net surplus and/or shareholders' account;

- partnerships: declared capital, net surplus and shareholders' account;
- limited partnership: declared capital and/or limited partners' account, net surplus;
- limited partnerships with share capital: subscribed capital, limited partners' account, official reserves, internal reserves, write-up balances;
- limited and joint-stock companies: subscribed capital, official reserves, internal reserves, write-up balances.

With the following meanings:

- net surplus: the difference between assets and liabilities;
- shareholders' and partners' account: the costs actually paid including contributions or profits or fees not withdrawn to be paid to unlimited partners. It is necessary to know the recipients' names and whether these costs are interest-bearing or not;
- declared capital: the official capital of non-stock capital companies;
- subscribed capital: the official capital of stock capital companies, including the various types of shares (ordinary, preference, deferred, etc.). If the capital is not paid up, it is necessary to know how capital call or increase are regulated; any missing share shall be included in 'financial fixed assets' or 'various receivables' according to whether its payment is on a short or long term;
- official reserves: these are shown in the published balance-sheet under different names;
- internal reserves: although these are not shown in the published balance-sheet, their numerical expression is included in the financial statement provided to us with clear names. The extent of internal reserves must obviously match the total of the actual higher values and be commented in the additional remarks to the balance sheet.

***Memorandum accounts and clearing entries:***

Third-party goods at the company premises or company goods at third-party premises (memorandum accounts), or potential third-party risks and liabilities on the company's behalf or company risks and liabilities on third-party behalf (clearing entries). These include:

- company securities deposited at or given for guarantee to third parties, whose extent is to be commented;
- company guarantees to third parties: this item always needs to be commented, for the risk that they may turn into bad debts, especially if given to other group member companies; signatures are often granted – sometimes mutually – to group companies in view of obtaining loans from the group;
- third-party guarantees to the company: it is necessary to know whether the underlying transaction is payable or next to become payable;
- derivatives: these include a number of contracts (swaps, futures, options etc.) for the hedging of financial risks or for speculation purposes. Special attention must be paid to these instruments, because they may involve significant potential losses.

***Non-recorded commitments:***

The most typical among these risks and commitments derive from:

- enlargements in progress, to be commented with the item 'fixed assets';
- purchase contracts and commitments. Their existence becomes clear from credit line opening, currency advance payments, trade advance payments, issue of guarantees, etc.;
- forward sales, that sometimes conceal disproportionate speculations;
- added value;
- promissory notes.

CHAPTER 9

# Debt Collection

*One of the important pillars of the trade credit insurance policy is debt collection in case receivables remain outstanding after due date of the invoice. Insurers require from their insured a good credit management and monitoring of outstanding receivables. This is of course in the interest of any supplier of credit, whether credit insured or not. Unpaid invoices can have a serious impact on the insured's turnover or cash flow.*

As soon as the insureds become aware that a claimable event is imminent or has actually occurred, they are obliged to take all necessary or expedient actions and to exercise all due diligence to avert or to mitigate the claim. This includes in particular drawing down securities, exercising his rights to retention of title and, if necessary, taking court action to recover the receivables. In doing so the insured is obliged to follow the insurer's instructions and to obtain the insurer's prior consent before concluding any composition arrangements, agreeing to payment schemes or entering into similar agreements.

The credit insurer expects the insured to conduct its buyer monitoring as if the credit were not insured. This means that it is expected the insured will spring into action if the invoice is still unpaid after the due date. Payment reminders should be sent to the buyer and/or phone calls should be made. This way possible disputes or complaints about deliveries can be detected in an early stage.

Most policies give the insured the freedom to continue deliveries despite the outstanding invoices, realizing that few buyers have the habit of paying their bills in time. This grace period is usually called the maximum extension period, and it starts on the due date and ends 30, 60 or 90 days later depending on the policy conditions. The variable duration of the maximum extension period can be related to the specific country, sector or financial status of the buyer. Continuing deliveries during the maximum extension are of course subject to a sufficient credit limit.

## DEBT COLLECTION BY INSURER

As an additional benefit, many credit insurers offer a debt collection service, which can render valuable assistance especially via partner agencies in other countries. When the insured's collection efforts have had no success, more serious action is required. In many policies the insured is obliged to hand over his outstanding invoices upon expiry of the maximum extension period plus 30 days (again, depending on the individual policy conditions). This means that cover (for any new transactions) ends at the expiry of the maximum extension period and that the insured must transfer all outstanding invoices to the insurer's debt collection service (including the ones that are not due yet) at the latest 30 days after the expiry of the maximum extension period. Of course the insured is free to do this earlier and, technically, as early as the due date of the invoice, although such an early action might damage the commercial relationship with the buyer. Some commercial flexibility is needed when supplying credit to the buyer and credit insurance is a helpful tool for this. For the insured it is reassuring that within the maximum extension period, he has the liberty and discretion to decide when to transfer collections.

## WHY DEBT COLLECTION BY THE INSURER?

Some policies do not carry the obligatory transfer of invoices for collection to the insurer for compelling reasons (e.g. collection done by an agency with specific expertise and knowledge in a certain trade sector). But usually this obligation is an integral part of the credit insurer's policy for the simple reason that the insurer is the risk bearer and therefore wants to determine how and when the collection will be conducted with the ultimate goal having better collection results and thus minimizing losses. The latter of course is in the interest of both parties: for the insurer there is lower indemnification and for the insured fewer claims could mean a positive effect on his premium (bonus/malus).

Another reason why the insurer might want the outstanding receivables transferred for collection is that, once a buyer is in default in payments, it is likely that several insureds with the same insurance company will report payment problems on this buyer. The insurer will bundle the claims of the different insureds, gaining a stronger negotiation position, and will prevent the buyer from playing off insureds against each other. Also, possible payment schedules agreed upon by the buyer and the insurer on behalf of the insureds can be monitored more easily.

A letter of demand for payment sent by the insurer may have more impact on the buyer than the requests done by the insured since the insurer could (threaten to) withdraw all credit limits belonging to other insureds whether overdue or not. Such intervention by the insurer usually depends on the level of the overdue account. If this approach leads to nothing, and all amicable efforts are exhausted, it will be necessary to take legal action.

## LEGAL ACTION

In order to take legal action the insurer needs some necessary documents: copies of invoices, order confirmations, letters of demand and all other correspondence related to the debt collection efforts done by the insured. Also a form is needed, signed by the insured, which authorises the insurer to proceed on behalf of the insured and to take all required steps in order to recover the outstanding monies.

If the insurer decides not to take recovery action, the claims with all the data are immediately sent to its partners that are involved in debt collection, which could be collection agencies (sometimes affiliated to the insurer) or lawyers. In the case of international collections, one is confronted with extra obstacles such as different languages, different habits and different legal systems and laws. A reassuring factor is that these collection partners are familiar with both the local system and customs and the working method and expectations of the insurer. They will try to secure payment or arrange a payment schedule but if these efforts fail they will start legal action with the local courts in order to obtain a court order. Execution of the court order will either lead to a payment or to the buyer's insolvency (declared legally bankrupt), which means that the claim can be indemnified. If execution of the court order is successful, the insured will be paid by the buyer through the collection partner and it is likely that the insurer will reinstate cover on the buyer.

It is of important to note that after the transfer of the file for collection, the buyer does not work directly with the insured any longer. Instead, all correspondence, contacts and possible money transfers should be directed towards the insurer and the collection partner. Nevertheless, if the buyer fails to do so, the insured should refer the buyer to the proper contact persons and payments received directly from the buyer by the insured should be reported immediately. If this rule is not strictly followed, it will lead to delay in the collection process and may lead to miscommunication among the parties to the detriment of the interests of the insurer and the insured.

## COLLECTION COSTS

Most collection agencies work on the basis of no cure no pay meaning that the agency makes money only if the collection is successful. In that case the agent will take a percentage of debts successfully collected, which can range from 10%–50% depending on the type of debt, age of the account and the country. The agent will try to recover these collection costs from the buyer, if possible and if allowed by local law, but often they remain outstanding and the insured will be charged.

This brings up another advantage of credit insurance, that many policies will cover collection costs associated with the full principal amount unpaid by the buyer even if the insured amount of an approved credit limit is lower.

One thing to bear in mind is that with a credit insurance policy, the insured's hands are not completely tied by the policy stipulations. An insured has the liberty of not abiding by the rules (e.g. exceeding the credit limit or continuing shipments after expiry of the maximum extension period) but this can have consequences for a possible future claim indemnification. Likewise, if the insured decides not to hand over the outstanding receivables for collection in time (e.g. to avoid adversely affecting the relationship with the buyer or because of other commercial reasons), they cannot be forced by the insurer to do so. Again, though, it is likely that this will have a negative impact on the claim assessment by the insurer since, by late action or no collection intervention, the insured has not helped in minimizing the loss and may have instead increased the risk. The same concern would apply to a situation where the insured decides to continue shipping at its own risk after a credit limit has been refused by the insurer. The policy cannot prevent the insured from shipping but, in case of default by the buyer, they are not entitled to claim reimbursement and, as well, collection costs would be for their own account.

## DISPUTES

A reason for non-payment by the buyer can be a dispute, which means that the buyer does not want to pay its debt, rather than the buyer is incapable of paying its debt (due to insolvency or some other reason). Thus, the shipment of incorrect goods or complaints about product quality can lead to disputes and have non-payment consequences.

Credit insurance covers non-payment only as a result of insolvency or protracted default. So in the case of a dispute, the insurer will suspend the insured's right to indemnification until the dispute is resolved. Since the burden of proving a claim rests with the insured, the best approach is for the insured to try to resolve the problem amicably to avoid damage to its long term commercial relationship with the buyer. If this does not lead to a satisfactory solution, the insured will need to take recourse through an arbitrator or in court in order to have the buyer's obligation acknowledged as legally valid and enforceable. Once the arbitrator or court has ruled in favour of the insured, they are again entitled to indemnification under the insurance policy.

Even in cases of disputed and thus uncovered invoices there can be an advantage to having credit insurance. Some buyers who are in financial difficulty raise a 'dispute' in order to delay their payment obligation by quibbling over trivia. Since in reality such buyers are short of cash it is to be expected that they will raise 'disputes' with many of their suppliers. If it happens that these suppliers also have a credit insurance policy, it is likely that the insurer will act pro-actively, as one dispute is plausible but to have several disputes with different insureds simultaneously is not, and so it will then be obvious that the buyer is financially disabled. For this reason, insurers will recommend that insureds report non-payments caused by disputes even though the invoices are not (as yet) covered In such a situation the insurer may take the initiative by requesting all insureds to hand over their outstanding invoices for collection immediately. By bundling and representing all claims of the several insured, the insurer will be in a strong position to refute the 'disputes' and hopefully recover the monies by swift action before the buyer becomes insolvent.

If the insured is confronted with a genuine dispute with which they do not agree, and the need for collection, it would be sensible to make use of experts within the insured's and buyer's industry. This could be an arbitrator, a lawyer of an industry organization or the insured's company lawyer. To have the collection procedure handled by the insurer would probably not be advantageous in these cases as it could lead to delays given the relative inexperience of the insurer's collection partner with technical aspects of the insured's industry and the potential for large volumes of correspondence needing to be exchanged.

A successful and quick collection procedure will prevent losses and sees to it that an insured does not have to go through the process of filing a claim. But in policies that also cover against protracted default it is very possible that the collection procedure is still running after a claim is paid. Depending on the judicial systems, in some countries it may take years before it is clear whether the collection efforts are (partly) successful and whether (part of) the outstanding invoices are recovered.

CHAPTER 10

# Imminent Loss and Indemnification

*A trade credit insurance policy provides the insured with cover*

- *for the non-payment risk;*
- *for insured debts;*
- *against insolvency of the buyer;*
- *provided that all policy conditions have been complied with.*

*According to the policy conditions the insured has to notify unpaid debts with a certain timeframe and ask for intervention of the insurer to collect the debt. The insurer will assess whether the insured has complied with all policy conditions and is eligible for cover and start the debt collection. In case all policy conditions have been met, indemnification will be made to the insured after the occurrence of a loss as described in the policy and the debt collection will be pursued, if possible. The indemnification and the allocation of recoveries will be dealt with at the end of this chapter.*

## THE NON-PAYMENT RISK

The supply of goods or the rendering of services on credit terms implies the risk for the supplier that payment will not be made in due course, and a loss occurs. This is the non-payment risk which can be divided into:

- the *pre-credit or production risk*: the risk that an order has to be cancelled during the production of goods, because the risk of non-payment due to financial problems of the buyer is too big; production costs already incurred cannot be recovered;
- the *commercial risk*: the risk that the buyer cannot pay the outstanding debt because of financial problems;
- the *country risk* or *political risk*: the insured does not receive payment of the outstanding debt because of political circumstances such as shortage of foreign currency, (civil) war, strikes, political unrest, natural disasters or non-payment by governmental buyers such as ministries, provinces, & municipalities.

Trade credit insurance provides cover for the above mentioned risks. One of the conditions for cover is that the debts qualify as insured debts.

## INSURED DEBTS

The conditions of a credit insurance policy may include an explicit description of the causes of loss that are eligible for cover (positive risk description) or the causes of loss that are excluded from cover (negative risk description). Some policies contain a combination of both.

Although policy conditions of different insurers vary, the common approach is that insured debts relate to a delivery or shipment or rendered services with the following conditions:

- within the scope of activities as described in the policy;
- a credit limit was in force during the delivery, shipment or the rendering of services;
- executed during the duration of the policy.

Of these debts only the net invoice amount including transport, insurance and packaging qualifies for cover. Other components such as VAT, cash discount, interest on overdue accounts and penalties are normally not eligible for cover (although some policies may include VAT as an insured debt).

Uninsured debts relate to a delivery or shipment or rendering of services:

- to a foreign governmental or public buyer (unless the political risk is also insured);
- to a private individual;
- to an associated company;
- for which the payment is made by an irrevocable letter of credit confirmed by a bank in the insured's country;
- paid in cash or by advance payments;
- to a buyer for whom a credit limit has been refused or fully withdrawn at the moment of delivery or shipment or services rendered;
- to a buyer located in a country not included in the policy.

Upon notification of the outstanding amount the insurer will determine if the debt is insured and covered.

## INSOLVENCY OF THE BUYER

Under a credit insurance policy the insured is entitled to indemnification of debts after the occurrence of an insured cause of loss due to non-payment: the insolvency of the buyer.

Insolvency occurs when a buyer cannot fulfil his payment obligations, because

- the buyer has been declared bankrupt;
- the acceptance of a scheme of arrangement for debt settlement has been sanctioned by the court;
- an extrajudicial compromise has been arranged with all creditors, or
- such conditions exist as are, by another system of law, substantially equivalent in effect to any of the above mentioned conditions.

Furthermore most insurers also cover protracted default. This occurs when payment of the outstanding amount has not been received by the insured after a certain period following the due date (called the waiting period) because of financial difficulties of the buyer or the country of the buyer. The length of the waiting period may vary per insurer.

However, it deserves attention that for insurance cover it is required that at the occurrence of a cause of loss the buyer cannot pay the debt. When payment fails to occur because the buyer is not willing to pay for reasons of dispute such as the amount of the debt or the quality of the goods or services, the indemnification under the policy will be suspended until the dispute is resolved in favour of the insured, either by arbitration or by a final court decision, binding both parties and enforceable in the buyers country. Only buyers who are incapable of paying are covered and not buyers who are not willing to pay. When buyers are not willing to pay, a dispute has occurred.

In addition compliance with all other policy conditions is required.

## OBLIGATIONS OF THE INSURED

In order to be covered, the insured has to follow several rules:

a) upon delivery, shipment of rendering of services there should be a **sufficient credit limit on to the buyer concerned**, be it a valid discretionary limit or a credit limit set by the insurer;
b) exercise an **active credit management** which includes
   - the applicability of conditions of delivery, including retention of title if required;
   - timely invoicing, mostly within 30 days after delivery, shipment or the rendering of services;
   - not agreeing with the buyer to longer payment conditions than the maximum credit terms stipulated in the policy;
   - sending regular payment reminders to the buyer and serving notice upon the buyer before the request for intervention;

- notifying the insurer immediately in case of adverse information such as a deterioration of the payment morality, unpaid bills of exchange, debt collection measures, but also the request of the buyer for extension of payment or an amicable settlement;
- taking necessary measures to minimise the loss in consultation with the insurer such as the stopping of deliveries, shipments and rendering of services as well as the exercising of all possible rights and securities;
- observing the same due diligence and prudence as if the debts were not insured.

c) give the insurer a **timely notification of overdue accounts or imminent loss with the request for intervention**: by a timely notification the insurer will be able to take measures to prevent or minimize possible losses such as withdrawal of credit limits and the start of debt collection against the buyer. A complete notification normally consists of
   - the notification form and the request for intervention;
   - copies of outstanding invoices and credit note's (if any);
   - a payment history of the buyer: a survey of all transactions (invoices and payments) with the buyer concerned during the last 12 months;
   - copies of all other relevant correspondence with the buyer.

**When should the insured give notification of a debt to the insurer?** Notification should take place in case of

- adverse information as described above under (b);
- expectation of the buyer's insolvency;
- an overdue account that remains unpaid after expiry of the term for notification mentioned in the policy;
- a special instruction by the insurer linked to the credit limit, requiring an earlier notification than allowed for in the policy.

d) make a timely declaration of the insured's whole turnover or outstanding debts and pay the related insurance premium in time: upon expiry of the period agreed to in the policy (every month, quarter, half year or year) the insured declares to the insurer the total insured turnover, i.e. the total of all insured debts.

## EXAMINATION OF THE NOTIFICATION BY THE INSURER

When the insurer receives a notification, they will assess whether the insured has complied with all policy conditions. This examination is made to determine the position of the insurer and to clarify to the insured their possible rights on indemnification. This examination may result in the assessment that there is no right or only a partial right of indemnification.

The notification will be examined for the following aspects:

***a) Completeness:***

In the absence of necessary documents, the notification cannot be processed. The required documents will enable the insurer to calculate the amount of the outstanding debt and to start the debt collection on the buyer. When the submission of these documents takes too long, this may have a negative effect on claim indemnification if the interests of the insurer was damaged due to delayed debt collection efforts or impossibility to minimize the loss.

***b) Whether the debt is insured or not:***

As already described, the policy conditions stipulate which debts are eligible for insurance or excluded from insurance. This results in examination whether

- the description of the delivered or shipped goods or rendered services as mentioned on the notified invoices matches the insured activities mentioned in the policy;
- the buyer is located in a country which is included in the policy;
- deliveries, shipments of rendering of services took place during the duration of the policy and not before inception or after expiry of the policy;

- the buyer is not a governmental institution (unless the political risk is insured) nor a private individual or an associated company;
- there were no shipments after expiry of maximum extension period;
- there was a valid credit limit.

***c) Timely notification of the debt:***

Unpaid debts have to be notified to the insurer with a request for intervention within the term for notification mentioned in the policy. When a debt is notified too late it is not eligible for cover under the policy. Not only are the notified outstanding invoices examined for timely notification, but by checking the buyer's payment history with the insured it will be determined if all past invoices were paid on time and whether there had been any other overdue accounts which had to have been notified to the insurer. In cases where an overdue account was not notified, the insurance cover does not apply to any debts arising after the date the earlier non-notified debt became overdue.

***d) Sufficient/adequate credit limit:***

The identity of the buyer owing the notified debt should be the same as the company for which the credit limit pertained. Furthermore, the credit limit should be valid and sufficient at the date of delivery or shipment of the goods or the rendering of services related to the outstanding debts. When it appears that there was no valid credit limit in force at the time of delivery or shipment of goods or rendering of services, the insurer will decline cover of the debts with respect to these delivery or shipment of goods or rendering of services. It is also possible that only a part of the outstanding debts does not qualify for cover, because the credit limit had been exceeded or the delivery or shipment of goods or rendering of services took place before or after the period that the credit limit was in force.

***e) The payment condition on the invoice:***

The payment condition – the period of time agreed upon with the buyer, within which the debts have to be paid – may not exceed the maximum payment condition approved in the policy. In case this is exceeded, the debt is not insured.

***f) Maximum invoicing period:***

In the policy the maximum invoicing period is stipulated. This is the period as measured form shipment or delivery date in which the buyer has to be invoiced. (It may happen that goods are shipped prior to the invoice being issued.) Exceeding this maximum invoicing period means that the debt is not covered.

***g) Insurance of the pre-credit risk:***

The insurance policy may also provide for cover of the costs made for the production of orders before delivery or shipment. This applies to the loss sustained by the insured after commencement or after completion of orders which cannot lead to supply or shipment of the goods because of the buyer's insolvency.

It is important that a sufficient credit limit was in force at the moment of acceptance of the orders. Furthermore, the period between the commencement of the execution of the order and the planned delivery or shipment may not exceed the maximum pre-credit period stipulated in the policy. Finally only the costs of the order are insured and not the intended invoice amount.

In case the insurer withdraws or decreases the credit limit before delivery or shipment, although the buyer is not insolvent, he has to instruct the insured and indicate whether the production of orders should be stopped or continued. In case of stopping the production, the buyer may start legal proceedings because of breach of contract by the insured. The policy conditions with respect to the pre-credit risk should make clear whether the consequences of the liability of the insured are covered or not.

When the examination results in a (partial) decline of cover the insurer shall inform the insured in writing as soon as possible. This is to prevent a wrong perception by the insured of possible indemnification on future losses, and to inform the insured about the debt collection costs that now will be for their own account and thus the need to minimise losses by starting its own debt collection process.

## THE REQUEST FOR INTERVENTION BY THE INSURER

***Debt collection by the insurer***

Usually the insurer will take care of the collection of notified debts in order to be in charge with respect to measures to be taken to prevent possible losses that have to be indemnified. Moreover, the insurer may avail itself of an extensive international collection network and, in case more debts are owed by the buyer to several insureds, to combine debt collection files and have a stronger position. The insured has to formally authorize the insurer to collect the debt when notifying the imminent loss.

***Serving notice upon the buyer before the request for intervention***

Before a request for intervention, the insured has to see to it that the buyer has been dunned already several times following the due date of outstanding invoices by means of an active dunning procedure both by telephone and in writing. The last written correspondence sent by the insured is meant to serve as a legal notice upon the buyer stating that in spite of several dunning letters no payment has been received and that the file will be transferred for debt collection unless payment will be received within a prescribed period. This letter will usually be sent to the buyer by registered mail and announces the involvement of a third party to do the collection – which has expense consequences – as well as to make clear in possible later legal proceedings what was required from the buyer.

***Power of attorney to collect: debt collection policy, costs and loss minimizing measures***

After the authorization by the insured, the insurer will determine how and by which means to proceed in the debt collection process. This applies to insured debts as well as to partially insured debts. Debt collection costs with respect to insured debts remain for the account of the insurer. In case the debt is not fully insured, according to some insurers the debt collection costs will be divided pro rata parte between the insurer and the insured. The insurer will inform the insured about this in writing.

In case the buyer contacts the insured directly in respect of payments or with a proposal for an extension of payment, the insurer has to be informed immediately. No promises can be made to the buyer without prior written consent of the insurer. The insured is obliged to take all measures in order to minimise losses and follow the insurer's instructions.

The insurer may instruct the insured to fetch back the delivered or shipped goods and sell them to a third party in case of an imminent bankruptcy of the buyer. Therefore it is necessary, if possible, that the insured has stipulated a strong retention of title in the conditions for sale and delivery. The deficiency thereof may lead to an infringement of the insurer's position with respect to the collection of the debt and consequently to a rejection of cover.

In a situation of imminent loss and in case of orders insured as a pre-credit risk, the insurer may instruct the insured to either supply the goods or try to resell the goods to a different buyer. This may not be easy in practice because the goods produced for the original buyer may be tailor-made and not easily sold to a third party.

Non-compliance by the insured with the insurer's instructions may have negative consequences for cover, because of the worsening of the possibilities for recourse.

***Disputed debt: no debt collection and suspension of cover***

During the debt collection procedure the buyer may dispute the debt. A dispute occurs when there is a disagreement between the insured and the buyer about the amount or the correctness of the debt or about the goods or services. Such a disagreement is also called a dispute.

In case of a disputed debt the insurer usually will abstain from debt collection or stop the collection which already has started. The insured will have to solve the dispute amicably, by arbitration or legally. The insurer will suspend cover and only indemnify after dispute is resolved in favour of the insured by arbitration or by a final court decision, binding both parties and enforceable in the buyer's country.

## THE CAUSES OF LOSS

***Insolvency and protracted default***

Some policies exclude losses arising from

- war between two or more of the following countries (China, France, Russia, United Kingdom, United States);
- natural disasters;
- nuclear explosion or contamination which may limit the extent of cover of insolvency and protracted default;
- causes of loss occurring in third countries (not the countries of insured or buyer), unless these countries are included in the policy;
- exchange rate fluctuation and devaluations;
- any general moratorium declared by the authorities of the buyer's country or by the authorities of any other country, through which payment must be effected;
- any other measure or decision by the authorities of a country, which wholly or partially hampers the execution of a sales contract;
- any political event or economic difficulty arising in a country, or legislative or administrative measure taken in a country, which prevents or delays the transfer of the sums paid by a buyer or his guarantor (transfer risk).

The insurer will have to prove that the insolvency or the protracted default was caused directly or indirectly by an excluded cause of loss.

In case of pre-credit risk cover, the definition of insolvency remains unchanged. Protracted default, however, relates normally to a due date following which the waiting period will start. Since there is often no due date before delivery or shipment of completion of services, some insurers change the wording of protracted default, and in the pre-credit situation in which the buyer could not accept the goods or services on the agreed date, the waiting period for indemnification will start from that redefined date.

## INDEMNIFICATION

The policy describes when indemnification will take place. In case of insolvency of the buyer or after expiry of the waiting period, the insurer must pay the indemnification usually thirty days after the insured has fulfilled all his obligations with respect to the claim. This includes the submission of all required data and documents and the transfer of the debt with all rights and securities attached to the insurer.

In practically all cases the insured will participate in the loss. This arises from the percentage of cover mentioned in the policy, and/or a different form of risk participation such as aggregate first loss deductibles, or an each-and-every type loss per buyer, or a threshold for qualifying claims.

## RECOVERIES

Before and after indemnification, the debt collection by the insured or the insurer may lead to partial payments. The allocation of these payments is stipulated in the policy.

Not every insurer treats the allocation of recoveries in the same way. Especially in case of exceeding the credit limit, or in case of partially uncovered debts, the rules for allocation may vary.

Recoveries received before indemnification may be allocated to the oldest outstanding amount.

Some insurers apply a pro rata allocation in case of partial cover.

Other insurers make a distinction between recoveries received before and after the prescribed date for notification of overdue accounts.

There are also insurers who distinguish between recoveries received before or after the occurrence of a loss.

Recoveries received after indemnification may be allocated to the insurer until the paid indemnification has been compensated. Other insurers may apply a pro-rata allocation for these recoveries.

Recoveries may take a long time to be received. Especially when debts owed by a country have to be rescheduled for a long period of time, the final collection of proceeds may take years.

CHAPTER 11

# Renewal, Expiry, Termination of a Policy

*Nothing lasts forever and that is also true for trade credit insurance policies. The policy becomes effective at the inception date and at the end of the insurance period decisions are to be taken with respect to (automatic) renewal, expiry or termination of the policy as well as the applicable conditions with respect to risks that commenced during the insurance period and did not yet lead to payment or indemnification.*

## RENEWAL

Most whole turnover policies include conditions for automatic renewal, which occurs at the end of the insurance period, unless the insurer or the insured wants to terminate the policy and notifies the contractual partner with due observance of a notification period of (mostly) two months.

The insurer may decide to renew the policy under the condition of an increased premium rate, because of the negative results under the policy, the deterioration of the creditworthiness of buyers and countries insured under the policy or the implementation of increased premium rates for all his buyers. After timely announcement of new (premium) conditions and a possible negotiation with the insured, the policy may be renewed or not.

Many policies contain a bonus/malus arrangement by which the insured can expect a decrease or increase of the premium rate, depending on the claims ratio of the policy. The calculation of the claims ratio requires special attention.

Under a 'risk attaching' policy the claims ratio should be calculated by taking into account the premium paid for credit risks commenced in an insurance period and allocating possible claims to the same period. Late indemnifications or recoveries may lead to an adjustment of the claims ratio and its consequences for the premium in a new insurance period.

Some insurers and many insured prefer a calculation of the claims ratio on a cash basis. Regardless of the insurance period in which the risks commenced, they take the premium paid during the last insurance period and the indemnifications paid in the same period, by some insurers decreased by the recoveries received by them during the last insurance period.

In case the insured is entitled to receive a bonus, one of the conditions may be that the policy will be renewed.

## EXPIRY

Under 'losses occurring' policies the decision to renew the policy is of influence for trade credit risks which commenced before renewal. Should one of the contractual partners decide not to renew the policy, the cover expires for trade credit risks outstanding after termination of the policy.

Policies without conditions for automatic renewal will expire at the end of the insurance period. Depending on the 'risk attaching' or 'losses occurring' character of the policy, the outstanding trade credit risks will or will not qualify for indemnification after expiry of the policy.

'Risk attaching' policies which include cover for the pre-credit risk should contain specific conditions for the continuation of cover after expiry of non-renewal of the policy. When the accepted orders do not lead to deliveries, shipments or completion of services during the last insurance period, and cover should remain in force, the insured still owes premium for these risks, although the policy has expired.

## TERMINATION

Some insurers reserve the right to terminate the policy immediately after a (covered) loss has occurred.

Policies will also be terminated before the end of an insurance period, when the insured becomes insolvent.

Non-compliance to the policy conditions and fraud may also lead to immediate termination of the policy, sometimes under the condition to remit indemnifications already paid. In those cases the premium already paid will not be remitted.

When one of the conditions of the policy may be a minimum premium per insurance year, the partial remittance of minimum premium already paid may be a legal obligation for the insurer, when the policy is terminated before the end of an insurance period. The costs paid at the inception of the policy or the insurance period for the (renewal of) credit limits are not to be remitted.

CHAPTER 12

# Single Risk Business

*The private political risk insurance market started developing in the early 1970s when international trade evolved from its historical bilateral structure into the multilateral format that led to the globalization we see today.*

*In those early days, import-export contracts with developing countries were mainly decided at the government level, and payments of such flows were secured by sovereign guarantees. This is why trade operators were said to be facing mainly 'political' risks.*

*With the trend towards privatization around the world in the 1980s and 1990s, buyers and sellers of traded goods increasingly were private (non-government) companies, and international trade rules were liberalized to the extent that government export subsidies became widely prohibited in the multilateral agreements involving private companies.*

This is why trade operators who had historically sought insurance protection against their 'political' risks also started seeking protection against commercial payment default by private buyers. The insurance market thus started to combine these political and commercial cover in the mid-1990s, and thus the term 'single risk' insurance was coined by most of the insurance providers.

## A FEW WORDS ABOUT TERMINOLOGY

Why 'single risk' and what does it mean?

The 'single risk' concept has been developed as a way to differentiate from the short term whole turnover (or portfolio) business that historically represented the bulk of activity of the credit insurance market. The diversity of international trade flows calls for such a differentiation.

On the one hand, sales of consumption goods occur by way of numerous regular deliveries to a large variety of buyers within the same country or throughout many countries. There is no specific commercial contract between the seller and the buyer for each and every delivery but rather trade is usually conducted pursuant to purchase orders sent by the buyer to the insured. Payment terms are agreed between the parties, generally on relatively short credit terms (ranging from cash-on-delivery up to one year credit). Short term whole turnover (or portfolio) insurance has been designed to cater to these trade flows specifically. On the other hand, sales of capital equipment or building/infrastructure construction or commodity trading are operated in a different way, frequently with commercial contracts written on a case-by-case basis, and exhibiting longer payment terms (tenors), and bank financing or other securities or collateral.

The single risk market is precisely addressing these types of trade flows, as well as the services contracts derived from these activities. However, it would be too restrictive to limit the perimeter of the single risk insurance market to the above transactions only.

Though belonging to the credit insurance branch, the single risk market also encompasses other types of international operations such as foreign investments – which may need to be protected against political risks, unfair calling of contractual bonds, trade or export finance contracts and structured finance contracts offered by banks.

Another, broader definition of the single risk insurance market might be given in a negative way: any trade operation that does not fit into the short term whole turnover (or portfolio) definition falls into the single risk category.

Rather than trying to find a comprehensive definition of the single risk concept, it may prove more accurate to try and list what are the main risks linked to each type of operation.

## INTERNATIONAL TRADE

- ***Export risks:***
  - contract repudiation or frustration which includes either the denial of the contract or its interruption or its cancellation, either by the buyer, private or public or by a government authority decision whether de jure or de facto (fait du prince);
  - contract interruption before delivery (pre-credit risk);
  - non-payment or protracted default or non-reimbursement of loans by the private buyer;
  - non-honouring of letters of credit;
  - embargo, withdrawal or cancellation of import/export license;
  - selective discrimination in law or regulation;
  - inconvertibility, non-transfer of currencies;
  - war, civil war, strikes, riots and civil commotion of political nature;
  - arbitration award refusal.

- ***Import risks***
  - contract repudiation or frustration as per above, including non-delivery of pre-financed goods and/or non-reimbursement of pre-financed sums;

- embargo, withdrawal or cancellation of export/import license;
- non-transfer of currencies;
- war, civil war, strikes, riots and civil commotion of political nature;
- arbitration award refusal.

- ***Contractual risks***
  - unfair calling of bonds (bid bond, advance payment bond, performance bonds);
  - enforcement of trade restrictions by the country of the seller.

- ***Investment risks***
  - confiscation of permanent or mobile assets;
  - expropriation;
  - war, civil war, strikes, riots and civil commotion of political nature;
  - non-transfer of dividends;
  - arbitration award refusal.

The single risk insurance market thus caters primarily to the needs of industrial or commercial companies having an international activity, including commodity traders and banks, since most of the transactions relate to capital equipment, construction/infrastructure projects or commodities trading – each of which generally call for financing. Over the last couple of decades, banks have taken on a growing importance in the insurance market, whether as loss payees or directly as insured. In addition to risk mitigation, banks benefit from the insurance capital relief as the regulatory or economic capital against an insured credit exposure is substantially lower.

While usually called the 'medium term' market because many of the insured transactions have maturities beyond one year, the single risk market also includes short tenor exposures, mainly in the commodities trading sector.

## THE INSURERS: EXPORT CREDIT AGENCIES (ECAs) AND PRIVATE MARKET

**Their characteristics:**

a) Historically single risk insurance has been a de facto monopoly of government agencies until the 'oil crisis' of the 1970s.

Until then, international trade and investment was operated mainly on a bilateral basis and frequently subject to government to government agreements. The ECAs had organized their operating rules and by-laws with limitations such as the obligation of 'national content' and rigorous insurance conditions to promote their national exports.

In case of claims, the community of creditors had organized a specific coordination tool, called the Paris Club, the role of which was to organize the rescheduling of public debts, mainly from the developing countries.

In such a context, there was not much room for a sound and sustainable private market involvement and it was generally considered that these risks, whether political or commercial were simply uninsurable.

b) The birth of 'the private market' goes back to 1969 – thus before the first oil crisis – at Lloyd's.

While buying marine cargo insurance, an exporter (insured) discovered that the Lloyd's policies included a 'waterborne' clause for war risks, which excluded protection when the goods were on land. The insured, nevertheless, wanted to cover their goods while in the port storage facilities against the risk of confiscation by the local authorities.

Most probably, the insurance underwriter who agreed to take this risk did not realize that they would be setting the rules of a political risk/single risk market that would continuously grow over the following four decades.

A few years later, international trade mechanisms changed substantially with the development of multinational companies and the growth of multilateral trade. This evolution represented a very attractive opportunity for private insurers since the ECAs were restricted to bilateral trade and the national content requirement.

A 'company' insurance market emerged in London with players that are now known as Atradius, QBE, Liberty Mutual or Axis, together with other Lloyd's syndicates stepping on board.

The US market developed during the 1970s with the progressive involvement of major players such as AIG (now Chartis), Cigna, Chubb, and then Zurich, Ace, Sovereign and HCC.

In Continental Europe, the first capacity was established in 1987 under the PARIS Pool. During the past two decades, new capacities were created with Unistrat (succeeding the PARIS Pool), ONDD, Zurich, Atradius, Euler Hermes, Garant, among others, and a few Lloyd's syndicates opening an underwriting office in Paris.

c) However, from the outset, the private market approach to political risks, becoming later single risks, has been quite different from the ECA rules.

- Having no constraint of national interest development, the private market focused immediately on the quality of the risks. This is the reason why the private market never pretended to be universal and has always been and remains selective. While the macro political or economic data remain an important element in the assessment of the risks, at the end of the day, private insurers make their underwriting decisions based upon the merits of each and every single transaction in the context of the given political and economic environment.
- Zero loss underwriting concept
- Private insurers, having seeing how large and costly the country debt reschedulings of the 1980s had been for banks, Multilateral Government Agencies and ECAs, did not want to enter into the same type of financial relations with the international buyers. They decided they would focus only on the contracts/projects that would represent a key interest for host countries, usually basic trade or investments. Though,

of course, there is always a degree of uncertainty in the political or economic developments within a country, such basic trade or investment flows would likely be the last to be interrupted in case of a crisis and the best-treated within the framework of a negotiated settlement. The zero loss underwriting concepts still inspire the market today, thus the very careful selection of risks by underwriters.

- Only companies (e.g. exporters, traders or investors) – more recently banks – having a credible internal risk management structure have a chance to find coverage in the private market. Such a statement appears normal nowadays but in the 1970s or even in the 1980s, it was a true revolution. Even more so, to give insured an incentive to reduce their exposures by themselves, private insurers had the idea to apply the premium rate not on the commercial contract value but to the maximum exposure at risk at any time during the life of the contract. In other words, the lower the risk at any time, the lower the insurance cost.
- One other key rule of the market results from this risk management requirement: the confidentiality clause. The 1980s 'debt crisis' had shown that neither banks nor ECAs were very well treated under international rescheduling agreements, being obliged to consent to very long repayment terms, if not debt forgiveness. Private insurers, with their accounting and reinsurance constraints, determined that they would be no better treated if they were entering into same type of 'syndicated-group' renegotiations and realized that, ultimately, a 'go-it-alone' approach by each individual exporter might avoid, under certain conditions, being caught into a 'group' approach by their buyers.
- Limited insurance capacity has also been a key feature of the private market in its early days and even through the first decade of this century. Because of capacity constraints, underwriters know that they will have to build up a portfolio of risks with a sufficient degree of diversity and avoid accumulation on

the same buyer, industrial branch or country, which could then be at stake in case of a single large political or economic event. But, at the same time, the capacity constraints and the aim to maintain a good spread in the portfolio causes underwriters to not write 100% of each individual risk that they may be offered – save for small contracts – and instead calls for risk sharing among various insurance companies, each of which can then offer a share of the total capacity needed. For the London market, having a long record of co-insurance agreements and syndication among insurers, it has been quite a natural move for its participants to share risks with one another, but it is interesting to point out that this companies' market in the US and in Continental Europe has spontaneously adopted a similar attitude. The private single risk market is indeed a risk sharing market.

- This is probably as well the reason why brokers have played such a prominent role in this market. Beyond 'organizing' co-insurance placements, they bear the important responsibility -as intermediaries – not only to inform their clients of the best possible insurance conditions in the market but also to help them in fulfilling their duties of full disclosure to the insurers. The link of confidence among insured, broker and insurer is crucial in assessing the risk and managing the policy and, in some cases, claims.
- Last but not least among the market characteristics: the determination of the insurance premium or cost. ECAs have a predetermined chart of premium rates, which is fixed in advance. Even more, under the umbrella of OECD (the Organization for Economic Co-operation and Development), an agreement has determined the minimum level of premium rate which should be applied by any Export Credit Agency on a country basis.
- The private market ignores this type of approach and would have refused it if contacted. Indeed the market keeps assessing risks on an individual basis. Further,

most jurisdictions prohibit premium rate-setting among insurance companies. In any case, there is no reason why the risk of a German exporter to a given emerging country would be the same as that of an Italian or Spanish exporter. And, if the risk is different, its price shall be differentiated accordingly.

Another difficulty comes from the inability to use traditional actuarial methods in setting the price of the risk.

All political events are different from one another. The fact there has been, say, a revolution with commercial consequences in a given country at a given period of its history does not allow predicting when a similar event would occur again and whether it would have the same magnitude. Building an actuarial sequence, in a business profile characterized by a low frequency of losses (i.e. the single risk market), in line with the drastic selection of risks, would not be a credible way to model the effective cost of the risks.

The law of supply and demand remains ultimately the most appropriate way for determining the price of the insurance. Based upon its own expertise, track record, portfolio profile and reinsurance costs, each underwriter shall determine case-by-case what is the minimum acceptable price in return for its insurance capacity.

## INSURING A RISK WITH THE PRIVATE MARKET

An exporter or investor that wishes to buy insurance in the private market will proceed gradually with three main phases: the application, the negotiation of the policy and the policy management. In case of a claim, three additional steps will have to be made: the claim declaration, the loss payment and the recovery process.

### *a) The application*

The formal application to single risk insurance is quite comprehensive.

However, underwriters have organized a fast and easy access for their clients:

- *Non-Binding Indication (NBI)*

Typically the applicant will first send the few key elements of their commercial contract or investment project.

- country of origin;
- country of the project or sales;
- name of the buyer;
- amount of the contract/project;
- estimated maximum exposure at risk;
- tenor;
- coverage requested;
- any element of experience, track record.

With these elements, the applicant will receive generally within twenty four hours (forty eight maximum) an NBI from the underwriters.

As defined, such an indication is not a committal for the parties but reflect the conditions of insurance that the underwriter would apply, once they would have reviewed all the required documentation to assess the risk in details. An NBI is theoretically valid for the time period specified therein: some underwriters specify a 48-hour validity period, whereas others may specify up to 30 days. In practice, it remains valid during the full negotiation process and, though non-binding, would not be withdrawn by the underwriter unless significant changes in the environment of the risk would occur in the meantime. Underwriters may, however, put a firm time bar for an NBI and require the applicant or their broker to ask for specific reconfirmation of the NBI once its period of validity has expired.

- In the NBI, the underwriter will indicate the basic element of their insurance conditions: insured percentage (see below uncovered percentage), waiting period (see below policy conditions), premium rate, maximum period of coverage and capacity (line) that they are prepared to put on the risk.

The NBI will also include 'subjectivities' defined by the insurer, which will require in the second phase the applicant to supply additional information.

- *The application form*
- A potential insured is held to the duty of disclosure. The concept has received various interpretations according to the different underlying legal systems (principle of utmost good faith in the common law environment). But due to the key importance in the risk assessment of the risk management operations of the applicant, the insurers will want to understand why the operator considers its commercial contract as 'acceptable' and how they intend to perform it. The single risk activity calls for a broad sharing of information between the two parties, insured and insurer, the aim being to have good knowledge of the risks. The expertise and experience of the applicant in managing their commercial contracts/projects will be one of the key aspects of the underwriting decision.
- From this standpoint, single risks widely differ from other insurance branches, where the insurer is considered as knowing the 'science' of the risk while the insured would be more ignorant. In single risks, it is of the utmost importance that the two parties reach as close as possible a mutual understanding of the underlying contract/project and the risks attached.
- The disclosure obligation is of paramount importance in the single risk activity. The implications of misrepresentation and/or reticence (whether deliberate or negligence) are different between the common law and civil law systems but may lead to cancellation of the insurance contract when it becomes obvious that the consent of one of the parties was obtained on the basis of wrongful or incomplete information.
- This is the reason why, if interested in the NBI received, the applicant will then complete a detailed application form, which will be attached to, and usually form part of, the

insurance policy. In addition to it, any other material, such as the commercial contract, terms of financing, details of any collateral, etc. will be sent to the underwriters for review.

***b) Negotiation of the policy conditions***

Once the applicant has accepted the terms of the NBI and the insurer confirmed its agreement on the principle to take the risks, the parties will negotiate the terms of the insurance contract. Indeed, in the single risk segment, standard wordings hardly exist and each insurance contract may be tailored according to the specifics of each underlying transaction. General conditions of the policy, frequently designed by the insurer according to the legal context under which the policy will work, remain usually unchanged. All the specifics of the coverage are defined in the special (particular) conditions, which, according to the rules of the contract, prevail over the general ones. This is the reason why the single risk market is renowned as being a tailor-made market, another reason for it not to easily fit with actuarial requirements and pre-formatted modelling.

The special conditions will determine some of the key elements of the insurance policy, such as the uncovered percentage or the waiting period and of course the definition of the law ruling the insurance contract.

The insurance wording shall include some basic conditions which remain in line with the risk management approach of the market:

- *Warranties:*
- the insured is committed to abide by all national and international regulations in the countries where the contract is performed;
- the insured must handle its operations in a careful manner and must take any step reasonable step to avoid or minimize a loss;
- the insured must not spoil the recovery rights of the insurer after a loss has been paid.

These warranties may be adapted in the main different jurisdictions but remain a core element of the relations between insurer and insured.

- *Exclusions:*

Private market wordings have a limited number of general exclusions which respond to three main concerns:

- not covering any action from the insured which may cause a claim;
- not covering losses resulting from events beyond control of the parties such as radioactive contamination or war involving the five permanent members of the security council of the United Nations;
- not covering losses covered by another insurance protection.

Indeed in the past decade, banks having become major buyers of single risks policies, it has been widely debated whether conditionality in the insurance wording would prevent banks from using insurance as a valid counterpart under Basel II regulations and several insurers have issued so-called Basel II compliant wordings. At the end of the day, it appeared that market wordings were no more conditional than those of ECAs and the new Basel III regulations are changing the approach.

The most important commitment taken by the insurers is the non-cancellation clause in the wording which gives the insured a strong degree of safety for the duration of their contract. It is a clause stating that given cover/credit limits will not be cancelled or withdrawn unless explicitly mentioned circumstances may occur.

- *Maximum exposure at risk*

The private market usually charges the premium rate on the maximum exposure at risk at any time. The insured is thus deemed to supply the insurer with an exposure chart, on a monthly or quarterly basis, and may require the premium to be calculated according to the said chart, generally on a quarterly or half yearly basis. The premium may be adjusted according to the real effective exposure which shall also be declared by the insured. The insured must assess their maximum exposure not only on the basis of their estimated credit against the buyer but also with the estimate of their costs in case of contract interruption or pre-shipment risk.

As an example, an insured having a 30 million contract over three years with three equal instalments will declare 30 million of exposure in the first year, 20 million in the second year and 10 million in the third year. If now the same exporter has a provision for three deliveries on a yearly basis, his maximum exposure at any time on the payment risk will never exceed 10 million. However, if such exporter has bought insurance for pre- and post-shipment risk, his maximum exposure in the first year will be 10 million (credit) plus X million representing the cost of manufacturing incurred during the first year for the second and/or third delivery. Similarly, if the insured wants to have the interest for payment delays covered during the waiting period, he must integrate that amount into the maximum exposure chart.

- *Premium*

In the single risk activity, the premium rate is applied to the maximum exposure at risk.

Whatever the tenor of the risk, the total premium is contractually due upfront. In practice underwriters frequently grant payment plans for the longest contracts but the full premium may be called immediately in the case of a claim. Only under the long investment insurance policies, do private insurers accept a payment on an annual basis, though it may generate complexities in the calculation of technical reserves. However, when insurers are covering multi deliveries of goods under the same contract (frequent in the commodity business), they shall then fix a minimum and deposit premium at the time of issuance of the policy and adjust such premium over time according to the effective exposure at risk during the lifetime of the insurance contract.

- *Uncovered percentage*

It has been a traditional practice in the market as with the ECAs that the insured should keep a portion of the risk uncovered as an incentive to participate actively in the claims and recovery process. Before the development of the market, ECAs would cover 85% of the contract value and leave 15% to the insured. This uncovered portion had to remain a risk for which the insured was not authorized to insure or discount elsewhere. With the evolution in the private market, the average uncovered portion has decreased from 15% to 10%, and below in certain circumstances or for some specific insured perils. As an example, in investment insurance, nationalization is usually covered 100% while expropriation would be covered up to 90%. The rationale behind this is that, in case of a nationalization law, there is nothing the insured can do in order to avoid or minimize the loss, while, for the other perils, he may have some room for negotiation.

A recent trend, emanating from banks' requirements and gradually accepted by the ECAs would push towards a further reduction of the uncovered percentage down to something between one and five per cent. One may doubt that the private market will follow this route en masse but it might become an additional criterion of coverage according to the quality of each individual risk.

- *Waiting period*

A 'waiting period' is also a traditional condition of any credit insurance policy.

There are many reasons for it:

* Need to ascertain that the claim is real.

In many cases, the payment default at due date is the result of neither the unwillingness nor the inability of the buyer to honour his payment duty but simply because of an administrative delay. In such a case there is no need to enter into the constraining process of claims and recovery, which may end up in a deterioration of the client relationship.

* Need by the insured to negotiate a settlement agreement.

Filing a loss with the insurance company may result in a conflict with the buyer. Most insured, when they think of the time and effort it took them to penetrate a country and build up a good client relationship, are keen to find an amicable solution with their buyer. In addition, as a consequence of the confidentiality clause, the insured remains on the front line with its buyer. Held to a duty of due diligence by the policy, the insured shall try to avoid a final breach of his business relationship with their local partner.

* Need to assess the validity of the claim under the policy (see below claims and recoveries).
* Need to assess the final value of the claim (see below claims and recoveries).

In addition to the waiting period, private market underwriters may also include a 'cooling off' period in circumstances where it is common knowledge that buyers never fulfil their duties at due date.

While the average tenor of waiting period is 180 days, it may go up to 360 days, to which may be added 90 or 120 days cooling off period.

*- Due diligence*

After full disclosure, due diligence is the second main obligation bearing on the insured. Here again, interpretation of the duties varies from one legal system to the other. In general terms, the insured is committed to take all reasonable measures to prevent or limit the occurrence of a loss and shall notify any aggravation of risk to the insurers while taking the necessary prevention initiatives to avoid or mitigate the loss. Though deemed to act on his own until a claim is filed, it is highly recommended to consult and coordinate with the insurers from the moment any such measures have to be undertaken.

*- Exclusions*

A single risk policy generally excludes some circumstances or factors, which cannot be insured and contains, mainly in the common law system, some warranties made by the insured

The main exclusions relate to the following aspects:

- radioactive contamination and nuclear occurrences;
- war between any of the five permanent members of the Security Council of the United Nations;

- bankruptcy or liquidation of the insured;
- non-respect by the insured of law and regulations relating to the performance of the contract;
- any peril which could be insured under a property insurance policy.

In the recent years, insurers have been asked to delete most of these exclusions, mainly upon request of banks in relation with the Basle II (and soon Basle III) capital rules. Some private insurers have drafted Basle II compliant wordings by limiting conditionality.

- *Warranties*

All single risk policies contain representations and warranties, whether in the Civil or in the Common law systems. Though their extent and limits may differ in these two legal environments, they are binding upon the parties and acknowledge their mutual understanding of either the context of the underlying transaction or the duties bearing on – or commitments made by – the insured in the performance of its contractual obligations under the commercial agreement.

- *Cancellation*

- A single risk policy is normally non-cancellable and the parties are bound until completion of the underlying transaction. This is an important difference with the short term whole turnover (portfolio) credit insurance where insurers have the right to reduce, suspend or cancel a credit limit during the life of the policy.
- In a single risk insurance, any deterioration of the risk must be reported by the insured to the insurer (due diligence) but the insurer may neither cancel the policy nor require measures that would not protect the interests of the insured in the same manner as it might protect the insurers.

- *Applicable law governing the policy*

Single risk business has historically mainly focused on international trade and investment with non OECD countries, though, with the recent sovereign debt crisis, there is now growing demand for risks in developed countries as well. The commercial contracts or agreement are thus ruled by a large variety of laws, the actual trend being that buyers or host countries are more and more requesting the commercial agreements to be ruled by their national law.

It would be simpler if the law applying to the insurance contract would be the same as the law ruling the commercial contract itself.

However, it must be acknowledged that the existence and development of bankruptcy and credit insurance laws in many countries are still at their early stages, while far more developed in other jurisdictions. Even in the OECD countries jurisprudence and legal doctrine in credit insurance is not yet highly developed everywhere and their limits may create additional risks to both insured and insurer. Moreover, because the single risk market is still fairly recent and does not generate a high frequency of claims, many courts in Europe have little experience in this field and lack references to make up their mind, once confronted with a litigation.

At the end of the day, single risks policies are operating these days mainly under three legal systems, the English and American common law in the UK and the USA, respectively, and the Civil law in Continental Europe.

***c) Binding the policy***

Though all the above steps are usually made rapidly, the time gap between the NBI and the binding of the policy may cause a problem of availability of capacity. As indicated above, in the single risk market, demand is generally bigger than supply. More specifically, when talking of certain highly demanded countries or buyers, underwriters, once their NBI has been accepted, may have to allocate their capacity on a first come, first served basis.

In such circumstances, it is advisable for the applicant to reserve the capacity in order to make sure it will be available the day it is needed. Such practice, rather frequent in the pre-2008/2013 crisis context, has been reduced during the past two years because new capacity has stepped into the market. However, when the applicant needs some weeks or months to finalize their commercial contract, they may prefer to have a certainty of the availability of the capacity and reserve it. In such a case, a reservation fee will be charged by the insurer, representing around 10 per cent of the estimated premium. The fee shall be reintegrated partly or in full into the premium, the day the policy is issued or will remain to the insurer in case the insured would finally decide not to buy the insurance.

***d) Co-insurance***

The true nature of single risks (amounts, tenors) has always called for co-insurance. When a risk had to be syndicated among several risk carriers, a policy leader was appointed in the policy. The leader would have defined the conditions of the coverage and generally would have the biggest share in the syndication. The leader, though consulting with the following lines, would as well make the decisions during the life of the policy, except in case of increased capacity needs, period extension or change in premium rate, where each participant would give a specific agreement.

In the recent period, a more extensive interpretation of a new requirement by the DG Competition at the European Commission, and endorsed by a growing number of brokers, might lead to a significant change in these good practices. Considering that traditional co-insurance agreement might be interpreted as a restriction in competition between market players, each underwriter would now have to indicate its own conditions when taking a 'line' on a given risk.

If the purpose is only to offer the insured a possibility to have each co-insurer offering its own premium rate for his own line, it may be practicable as long as such differences do not trigger diverging interests among co-insurers. If such differentiation should apply as well to other policy conditions (waiting period, exclusions, uncovered percentage), it would rapidly make the policy unmanageable by the insurers because, at the end of the day, when there would be a payment default, the insured would need to have a single negotiation with the buyers for the total amount due and not by tranches according to the specifics of each insurer's conditions. A key condition to the success of all claims negotiations with the buyer is to maintain cohesion and consistency between the insured and its insurers.

Creating artificially diverging interests among the parties at the time of underwriting would ultimately serve nobody's interests, except the defaulting buyer. Over years, sound practices have been set up with a lot of pragmatism by the market players. They must be protected as a guarantee of the reliability and sustainability of the private market.

***e) Claims and recoveries***

When confronted to a potential loss, the insured must take the steps stipulated in the insurance policy. The process shall be divided into three phases: the claim declaration, the loss indemnification and the recovery procedures.

*- Claim declaration*

As from the moment the insured is advised of the occurrence of one of the claim generating factors defined in the policy wording, they shall inform the insurers of such event, and provide all additional information regarding the circumstances, the amount at stake and the prevention or mitigation measures undertaken. From the date of such formal declaration, the waiting period will start running unless the insured specifically requires a delay to the start of the waiting period. During the waiting period, pursuant to its duty of due diligence, the insured will take any necessary steps to mitigate and avoid the loss.

At the same time, underwriters will, in most cases, appoint a loss adjuster, who will be in charge of reviewing all elements of the claim in regard to the policy conditions and assess the final amount of the loss. Due to the complexity of many underlying contracts and sometimes to travel on site to collect all the information, the loss adjuster will perform their duties during the waiting period and beyond if necessary, keeping underwriters regularly updated of the progresses of their findings.

Unless waiting longer would clearly result in an aggravation of the loss, underwriters will abstain, during the waiting period, from requiring the insured to take any step which might end up ruining the business relationship between buyer/buyer and seller.

- *Loss indemnification*

At the end of the waiting period, insurers are given 30 days in most wordings to proceed to indemnification of the loss as quantified by the loss adjuster and accepted by the parties. At the same time, insurers and insured must agree upon the terms of the subrogation act which shall be signed in parallel with the payment of the indemnity, even if subrogation is automatically conferred by law to the insurer in the legal framework under which the insurance policy has been bound. Interest for payment delays during the waiting period are normally not covered under the insurance policy unless first, they are included in the underlying contract and collectable from the buyer and, second, they have been integrated in the calculation of the maximum exposure and accepted by the underwriters as such.

- *Subrogation and recovery*

Once a loss is paid, insurers are subrogated in the rights of the insured to collect the amounts due by the defaulting buyer.

- However, in many countries, mainly outside the OECD, such a subrogation right might not be systematically recognized and could, for instance, conflict with a provision of the underlying contract by which the insured would not be authorized to cede any of its rights under the contract to any third party or would be subject to approval by the other party.
- Another element of complexity comes from the fact that insurers are subrogated to the rights of the insured up to the amount paid by them.

With the uncovered portion clause, the insured always keep a portion of the rights against the defaulting party. Meanwhile, it is rarely possible in the negotiations with the buyer to divide the debt between the insurers' and the insured's portion. In order to avoid any conflicting situation, the insured usually signs, in addition to the subrogation act, a mandate granting insurers all authority to claim for the full amount of the debt. Doing so, insurers are vested with all necessary authority to take the most appropriate actions in order to recover promptly the biggest possible portion of the loss.

- In practice however, because of the confidentiality clause, insurers will be reluctant to undertake direct action against the buyer and will, rather, grant back to the insured a mandate to act in their joint interest – and upon their instructions – towards such buyer.

As the insured is committed to suspend any further delivery to its defaulting client until a solution is found on such overdue, both insurers and insured find their interest in having the insured still in the front line.

- Only in cases where both parties would consider the 'appearance' of insurers towards the buyer as a 'good pressure' to help a solution, would insurers agree to participate on their own in the recovery negotiation/litigation.
- In the recovery process, insurers may ask the insured to take tough actions against the buyer and policy wordings include a clause by which insurers would be allowed to claim return of the indemnity in case they would be deprived by the insured of their recovery rights.
- *Recoveries have always played a major role in the private market*

From an economic standpoint, recoveries have been cited as representing up to 35 per cent as an average of losses paid by insurers. Would such recoveries not, or hardly, exist, insurance costs would have to be increased by almost 50 per cent, thus making it no longer competitive for insurance purchasers. In addition to this, some of the losses do not lend itself to any recovery. For instance, political violence claims could not be recovered, in addition to the loss of revenues, in the case of expropriation.

It happens, however, that there is a growing demand for these categories of risks. Market underwriters will have to check what percentage of such coverage they may 'tolerate' as part of their whole portfolio of risks.

On a more commercial side, recoveries are part of the long lasting and confident relation an underwriter may build up with his customers. An insured filing non-recoverable losses in the market might have difficulty finding support for their future contracts over time.

## REINSURANCE

Reinsurance has always played a key role in the single risk market. The individual size of some risks, and even more the concentration of exposures on some risk factors, call for an adequate dilution of portfolio risk for each and every direct insurer.

However, reinsurance capacities for single risk business have always been more limited when compared, for instance, to the short term whole turnover activity.

Several elements may have contributed to this relative reluctance:

- lack of knowledge about the rationale of such trade and investment flows;
- lack of a reliable track record at the market level;
- difficulty to use actuarial methods in evaluating risks;
- perception of single risk as being of catastrophic nature;
- different perceptions of the nature of 'political risks' in the early days;
- size of the market.

Since the beginning of this century, and much more with the 2008/2009 period, reinsurers are showing more appetite for this class of risks. Indeed the experience of the past thirty years has proven a low frequency of claims, an acceptable severity and a growth in demand and in the global size of the market.

It is important for the future of the single risk market that reinsurers continue deepening their expertise in this field and allow for an adequate diversification of each player's portfolio of exposure.

Despite the present difficulties in the banking sector, the world economy is bound to keep growing, pulled primarily by the emerging and developing countries. Demand for single risk insurance shall grow and evolve, maybe with an increase in medium term projects. The issue of accumulation will thus remain a major concern and insurers and reinsurers shall need to prepare to bring appropriate answers. Combining the various techniques of reinsurance shall certainly be part of such answers.

## CONCLUSION

Single risk business is a very special aspect of the credit insurance industry, and perhaps even throughout the whole insurance industry. Meanwhile, today, it plays a key role in international trade and investment.

Born from a pragmatic approach, it has developed mainly thanks to the initiative of each individual player. However, the rules and guidelines used by private market underwriters has influenced all other players and enhanced the risk management awareness by all actors involved in global trade and investment.

Thanks to its stringent technical rules, risk selection, portfolio diversification, risks dilution, the private market has, in 40 years, never been confronted with any total country or industrial branch loss, contrary to predictions otherwise from some observers.

International trade flows shall keep diversifying in the coming years because of the gradual entry of emerging countries into the supply chain. Trade between emerging countries, hardly existing two decades ago, now represents over 25 per cent of the total global trade flows. Many Export Credit Agencies have been established in the emerging and developing markets during the past 10–15 years. With the reduction of most national budgets, there is a move to more cooperation between the private and the public market for sharing risks, which are sharply increased. Many of the ECAs may not expect significant budget allocations from their government. It is not hard to predict therefore that private market insurers and ECAs will enter into a closer dialogue and will find interest in sharing risks among one another.

Because of the specific nature of the risks it covers, the private market should avoid being caught in the global trend of concentration which has prevailed in the banking and insurance sector since the beginning of the 1990s.

The 2009 crisis has precisely revealed that small capacities have performed at least as well as the biggest. The reason behind this is that reliability in this segment is not a consequence of size but much more of proportion. As long as each carrier maintains a good balance between its financial structure, its capacities and its portfolio of risks, the market will remain sound. Keeping a significant number of players helps maintain the necessary diversity in the various portfolios while any attempt to move towards standardization would inevitably lead to unsustainable concentration of risks.

Of course, some opportunistic players may from time to time try and penetrate the market with a short term vision. But, being in essence a long tail activity, single risk calls for long term investment in know-how and a permanent adaptation to the fast changing conditions in the international trade practices. Those who would not want to commit in the long run to the segment do generally not stay very long in this market.

In its own interest, the private market must, however, from now on take new initiatives to have its rules and best practices better known among the business community and beyond in the judicial circles.

The private market is still much less known than ECAs, whether in quantitative or qualitative terms.

More information about the private market shall facilitate the necessary dialogue between the two types of risk carriers and generate a bigger appetite on the part of the international trade and investment business community.

CHAPTER 13

# The Single Risk Insurance Market: Private and Public Players

## *PARTICIPANTS. A BRIEF INTRODUCTION*

*Research has shown the origins of trade credit export insurance in certain commercial transactions in Egypt, Mesopotamia and Rome. These were single transactions backed by a guarantor that obtained a commission for the service provided. Some additional information is to be found in Chapter 2.*

The definitive push toward a trade credit insurance market took place in the 1960s when the proliferation of credit in international transactions and the growth of domestic and export markets made it necessary to discover and develop mechanisms to protect against payment defaults.

The deferral of payment for the purchase of goods and services (i.e. extending credit) has on the one hand caused a significant increase of commercial transactions for many companies but, on the other hand, these same companies faced the threat of payment delays, extensions and bankruptcies that may seriously affect their own economic viability. Jean Bastin defines credit insurance as 'a safety system that allows creditors, after the payment of a premium, to be insured against the non-payment of credits due from specific corporations'. Professor Jacques Janssen goes on to state that '(credit insurance) is a contract on behalf of which the insurer guarantees the insured, through a premium, the payment of a certain amount in case of the occurrence of a certain risk.'

The three essential terms in this short definition are the premium, the amount insured and the risk insured.

## THE ROLE OF THE STATE

Exports are a large part of the GDP (private consumption + gross investment + government spending + (exports-imports)) of any country in the world. Over the last sixty years all OECD economies have tried to promote exports using various schemes, mainly involving financing and insurance. The other driver of the export growth is demand, which is derived from consumption, investment and government spending; however, each of these drivers have been adversely affected by the economic crisis of 2008–2012.

These factors, plus trying to balance the payments of each economy are the main reasons why, worldwide, different states are continuing to support schemes to boost sales beyond their borders. One such scheme with the most useful longest tradition is credit insurance. As we have explained, exports, financing and insurance are three corners of the same triangle.

After World War II many specialized companies were created by their respective countries in order to develop export credit insurance and the export guarantee programmes on behalf of the state. In the OECD countries these companies were known generally as Export Credit Agencies (ECAs) because although they did not give any credit (with the exception of Eximbanks), their own name was meant to denote that their main goal was the protection of the financer.

The ECAs developed several products to cover the commercial and political risk of international transactions but with a main separation: short term transactions and commercial credit were insured on their own behalf but the long term transactions and political risk were insured on behalf of each state. The European Union (predecessor), Australia, Japan, Canada, Korea, Norway, New Zealand, Switzerland and the United States, developed the OECD Consensus in July 1976. It consists of a group of international guidelines for handling official financial aid for exports. Since its inception there have been three goals:

- strengthen the transparency and discipline of official aid to promote exports inside each member;
- eliminate the character of subsidy for export of financial aid and
- avoid unfair competition between member states.

The OECD Consensus was termed 'a gentleman's agreement' but is mandatory inside what is now the European Union since 1978. Among other things, this implies that the signatories of the agreement have a common scheme for financial aid in commercial transactions having repayment terms equal to or longer than two years. The longest tenor is 10 years but with some exceptions may go for a longer period.

The Consensus developed certain procedures that have become standards in international trade operations:

- the interest rate charged to a buyer in a buyer credit-type transaction is called CIRR (Commercial Interest Reference Rates) (not libor or euribor) and is provided monthly by the OECD.
- there has to be an advance payment of at least 15% of exported goods and services.
- there is a limit in local expenses that may not exceed 30% of the exported goods and services.

Within these guidelines the ECAs have developed three main products:

- Supplier Credit Transactions: in this case, the risk covered is the non-payment of a private or public buyer. In case of a tender or a turn-key project, it is possible also to cover the fair and unfair calling of the standard bonds involved (bid bond, advance payment bond, performance or guarantee bonds).
- Buyer Credit Transactions: in this case the risk involved is the non-reimbursement of the credit granted by a local bank (country of the exporter) to the bank of the importer.

- Investment Transactions: in this case the only risk covered is political risks mainly confiscation, expropriation, nationalization and expropriation; non-payment or non-transfer of dividends due to legislative or administrative measures; and physical damage of assets provoked by a strike, a riot, a war, an act of terrorism or civil conflict.

## PRIVATE MARKET OF LONG TERM POLITICAL RISKS

The London Market, originally known as the Lloyd's market, has been operating since 1688 insuring any kind of trade risks but mainly transportation risks involved with commercial transactions.

Since the end of the 1980s, a private market was developed (non-regulated by the OECD consensus) outside the Lloyd's market and with the participation of new players, some existing ECAs, former ECAs such as Unistrat Insurance, private companies such as QBE, Zurich or Atradius. It is informally called the Companies Market.

It is important to indicate that inside the OECD, most of the ECAs were privatized, having now been taken over by private shareholders and managing the risk on behalf of the state, in some cases as a mandate as part of the takeover.

The existence of this private market is possible because it complements the public (state government) schemes. It should be kept in mind that since 2008 the OECD countries have enhanced their insurance cover for long term and political risk transactions (e.g. 99% coverage, unlimited capacity for certain countries, reduction of waiting periods).

The main reasons for using private market insurance are the following:

1. Transactions between six months and two years. Generally we speak of single risk transactions when these are not able to be insured either under the traditional whole turnover policy or via the long term supplier policies on behalf of the state.

2. Amounts not included in a buyer credit transaction: advance payment, local costs, non-national goods and services. In general the financing banks have developed what is called a commercial or complementary credit. 'Commercial' because the conditions granted, tenor, percentage of cover are more commercial than political; and 'complementary' because it complements the buyer credit facility.
3. The speediness of the response. An exporter that wants to present a tender in few days needs an urgent response.
4. Insurance flexibility. In the private market the insured can arrange for either standard policy wording or tailor-made wording, as may be needed. There are also some countries not covered by the ECAs but where the private companies may provide cover.
5. Need for capacity. In investment policies the capacity amount delivered by the public market may not be enough for the capacity needed, thus the need for co-insurance syndication among many companies (public and private).

## THE FUTURE OF THE SINGLE RISK MARKET

As we have noticed, the Political Risk Insurance (PRI)/single risk market exists because it fills certain needs of the international trade community not completely covered by public schemes. The 2008–2010 subprime crisis has brought an enormous demand for public (government) support in many economic aspects of corporate and bank business life, including trade finance operations. With the re-emergence of public services due to this hunger for risk mitigation products and with increased funding possible in this area, the PRI market should evolve to keep pace with the changes in the market, just like the public entities.

During the last few years, a typical example of collaboration between public and private schemes was under commercial credits in a buyer credit transaction, first insured via the ECAs and then later in the PRI market. The increase in the cost of funding has made banks reluctant to pay part of their margin as a complementary credit. This scheme maintains its validity but new ways of collaboration may emerge in the future.

Going forward, the private market can provide ECAs the knowledge and expertise of

- insuring private buyers worldwide under both export and domestic projects;
- taking risks of pre-and post-shipment, and unfair calling of bonds in the same program;
- cover for import projects: covering non-reimbursement of advance payments made to an insured that remains unpaid due to political risks;
- eliminating the commercial risk in the confirmation of a Letter of Credit.

Finally the 'Arab Spring' movements in 2011/2012 have brought an increased demand for foreign investments risks insurance.

- Loss of rights and assets: confiscation, expropriation, nationalization and expropriation of tangible or intangible property or equipment.
- Dividend non-payment/non-transfer: covering the non-transfer of dividends due to legislative or administrative measures.
- Physical damage: this guarantee covers assets in case of physical damage provoked by a strike, a riot, a war, an act of terrorism or civil conflict.

In 2001, few companies considered that Argentina could cause a loss to foreign investors due to non-transfer of dividends out of the country. History has shown that the lack of appetite for risk protection was misplaced and obviously did not match the default scenario that developed in the country. Nowadays, foreign investors demand the market to cover millions for investment risks. In general, no single risk player can take on all the risk capacity demanded by the market, so once again the public and private schemes may need to act together to provide the coverage required.

CHAPTER 14

# Reinsurance of Trade Credit Insurance

*Reinsurance is – simply stated – 'insurance of insurance'. In fact, most of the principles ruling insurance such as self-retention, etc. are common also to reinsurance. In this chapter we will look at the use of reinsurance in trade credit insurance, explaining more in detail some basic reinsurance principles and how they fit to trade credit insurance.*

*Why reinsurance? – Use and purpose of reinsurance*

*Reinsurance is a powerful instrument serving the following purpose: It absorbs losses and stabilises the insurance company's results, and by so doing, it effectively and efficiently acts as a capital substitute. By replacing capital, insurers are able to grow their business. How much losses the insurer wants to transfer to reinsurers and subsequently how much capital relief the insurer will obtain, will depend on its risk appetite and overall (regulatory, internal and rating) capital requirements.*

The importance and use of reinsurance varies according to the line of insurance business. 'Commoditized' insurance lines such as life insurance, household, motor, etc. generally require less reinsurance than 'Special' insurance lines such as agriculture, engineering and/or trade credit and surety. Why?

- *Limited access to outside capital*: Trade credit insurers have always been specialized insurance companies; besides the complexity of the product itself, high entry barriers and high sunk costs in establishing new 'greenfield operations' constitute big obstacles to potential competitors and to potential capital providers when it comes to financing the business. External sources of capital are therefore rare, so reinsurance can be considered being a suitable capital provider.

- *High degree of specialization*: The niche character of this business results in very few people having thorough knowledge about trade credit insurance outside of the insurance and reinsurance industry.
- *Low diversification*: Until 1990 trade credit insurers' portfolios were largely focused on their domestic boundaries: a German trade credit insurer would insure almost only domestic trade credit in Germany, a French insurer only French trade credit, etc. These portfolios would to a great extent follow their own country's economic cycle. As a consequence, whatever economic downturns affected one country (e.g. crisis of construction sector in Germany), the credit insurer's portfolio would immediately be hit, resulting in very high loss ratios. With lack of outside capital sources, the only way to efficiently absorb such high loss ratios was by way of reinsurance.

With increasing integration of world trade, elimination of regulatory hurdles and strong capitalization, trade credit insurers started to merge and diversify their own portfolios. This diversification has also contributed to a larger stabilization of results, more global players and a diminished use of reinsurance.

## TYPES OF REINSURANCE/OBLIGATORY REINSURANCE TREATIES

Basically, trade credit insurers make use of the two main types of reinsurance: Proportional and non-proportional reinsurance. Proportional reinsurance can be compared with 'whole-turnover' policies while non-proportional can be compared with excess of loss policies.

***a. Proportional reinsurance:***

The insurance company buys reinsurance protection for its complete portfolio of policies on a proportional (i.e. pro-rata or quota share) basis. The insurer cedes part of the premium income (e.g. 30%) and the reinsurer will pay the losses according to the agreed participation (e.g. 30%). This reinsurance type is suitable if the insurance company is seeking protection against 'frequency losses' or it expects to grow.

Global trade credit insurers that have grown significantly over the past few years, have been able to reduce their reinsurance to approximately 30%–50% of the total portfolio. This is still higher than in other lines of business. A Quota Share treaty, very often in combination with an Excess of Loss treaty (covering a portion of the insurer's retention under the quota share treaty), is the main type of reinsurance programme used by the major trade credit insurers.

Other types of proportional reinsurance are the variable quota share or the surplus reinsurance/surplus of lines. If the ceding company would like to limit their monetary retention, especially for the higher limits, it can buy a variable quota share treaty, i.e. it can agree with the lead reinsurer on a higher cession for buyers with limits above a certain threshold (e.g. retention/cession of 50%/50% up to a certain limit, and then above that limit – but not to exceed the overall maximum treaty limit – the retention/cession could be 25%/75%).

With a surplus reinsurance, the ceding company keeps all polices up to a certain limit in their retention and all limits above this level are then split between the ceding company and the reinsurer. If the ceding company thinks that it can afford to have a loss up to € 1,000,000 but the limit should be €10,000,000, the reinsurers would take 9 lines and the ceding company 1 line. The premiums and losses are split in the same relation. Surplus treaties are, however, rarely used in trade credit insurance as it is very difficult to handle in the credit insurance environment. Likewise, variable quota share treaties are rarely used in credit insurance due to the same reason.

***b. Non-proportional reinsurance:***

The insurance company buys reinsurance protection only for losses exceeding a certain amount (e.g. losses exceeding € 1,000,000 up to € 2,000,000), paying a pre-agreed premium amount which will be calculated as a rate of the expected premium income. This reinsurance type is suitable if the company feels comfortable about its 'normal' loss ratio but wants protection against severity losses affecting either its whole portfolio (pure excess-of-loss) or the part which remains un-reinsured (excess of loss on retention, i.e. the retention of the insurer arising from any of the above-mentioned proportional reinsurance).

Non-proportional reinsurance is not very new to trade credit insurers. The combination between proportional and non-proportional reinsurance is quite commonly used by all major trade credit insurers: while they are able to retain more business (i.e. use less reinsurance due to the reasons mentioned above), there is contemporaneously a bigger need to shift from capital substitution to capital protection.

Very selectively do trade credit insurers opt for additional reinsurance protection, with the last major event related to the Year 2000 ('Y2K') and its possible consequences.

***c. How is reinsurance protection bought?***

The number of market players in trade credit insurance and reinsurance is very limited and until some years ago, negotiations would have taken place directly between trade credit insurers and leading reinsurers, while the other reinsurers would have adhered to the pre-negotiated conditions. More recently, reinsurance brokers have gained a foothold. Trade credit insurers now seek more competitive conditions, while at the same time some established reinsurers reduce their offer and new reinsurers appear and are able to provide more competitive conditions. But what do both parties require?

Trade credit insurers look basically at

- the amount of capacity a reinsurer will be able to provide
- conditions the reinsurer will offer
- credit risk the reinsurer represents (i.e. financial rating of the reinsurer)

Capacity: In normal reinsurance language, 'Capacity' is what the reinsurer provides to the trade credit insurer, i.e. it is similar to the insurance cover provided by a trade credit insurer to its policyholders. In trade credit insurance, the insurance cover relates to a specific buyer on which the trade credit insurer will grant credit limits whereas in reinsurance, the reinsurance cover will just be expressed as one amount.

For a proportional quota share treaty, setting this amount, i.e. determining the amount of reinsurance cover, the credit insurer has to know its highest exposure. It is important for the credit insurer to have sufficient capacity for its exposures on each and every buyer/buyer group, i.e. the credit insurer has to calculate which buyer/buyer group has the highest accumulation of credit limits coming from the various policyholders in its portfolio.

A reinsurer does not have the resources and organization to perform the same level of buyer underwriting/credit assessment and monitoring as does a trade credit insurer; and therefore the reinsurer relies substantially on the trade credit insurer's (the 'primary insurer's') underwriting skills.

The following treaty structure (quota share) is very often used in trade credit insurance:

- *'Automatic' treaty limit*

The automatic treaty limit per buyer/buyer group in a proportional treaty is comparable to the 'discretionary' limit in trade credit insurance. This limit should be high enough to cover the majority of the exposures, i.e. this 'automatic' limit should allow the credit insurer to underwrite the biggest part of the credit limits per buyer/buyer group up to this amount.

- *'Special limit' for named buyers*

In order to achieve some control and to manage its portfolio, the reinsurer prefers to be involved with the largest limits for buyers/buyer groups. The credit insurer thus will have to provide information on those buyers/buyer groups that exceed that specific threshold level/automatic treaty limit.

The reinsurer will then analyse these 'named' buyers separately and, depending on the outcome of the analysis and the quality of the risk, the reinsurer will grant additional specific reinsurance cover and will set a special limit as the new, ultimate threshold. These buyers and their corresponding limits will then be separately identified by name ('Named Buyers' or 'Named Risks') by the trade credit insurer in its reports to the reinsurer.

For non-proportional treaties, setting the amount of reinsurance cover for trade credit programmes is somewhat more complicated. In normal reinsurance practice, non-proportional treaties are structured according to loss expectations and 'layered' (just like a corporate bond) according to its loss probability in 'senior', 'junior' and 'equity layers'.

What are the loss probabilities in trade credit insurance? Unlike mortality tables or burning cost factors used commonly in other lines of business, loss expectations in trade credit insurance will have to be determined on the basis of the available portfolio information, i.e. the insured amounts, the default probabilities of the buyers and the risk mitigation measures such as self-retention, retention on title, etc.

Conditions: Conditions and Terms – particularly financial arrangements that are driven by loss activity – are also a decisive factor when buying reinsurance. One condition which is, relatively unique to trade credit insurance is the 'commission', also known as 'ceding commission'. The commission represents what the reinsurer is willing to pay to the insurer for the business, i.e. to cover the acquisition/administration costs of the trade credit insurer. This is usually one of the hottest topics of negotiations because reinsurers do not necessarily have full transparency into the cost structure of the trade credit insurer and thus do not want to provide trade credit insurers with a commission that exceeds the trade credit insurer's effective costs. Commissions are usually expressed as a percentage of the reinsured premium volume.

The commission schemes negotiated with the trade credit insurers can reflect 'bonus-malus' elements. Considering the 'volatility' of the business, most trade credit reinsurance treaties contain such bonus-malus clauses whereby commission is a function of an estimated loss ratio (i.e. the higher the loss ratio, the lower the commission), or the commission is fixed at a very low level but then subsequently adjusted by a profit commission as add-on depending on the results of the trade credit insurer under the reinsurance programme.

Credit risk/counter party risk: Buying reinsurance is also a matter of 'confidence' or, more precisely, the credit risk the reinsurer represents – after all, the reinsurer should be stable enough to pay for losses to come in future years. Confidence and credit risk are not always synonymous. Trade credit insurers have to take into account the credit risk posed by reinsurers. Being experts in such matters trade credit insurers will usually seek protection from reinsurers rated at least 'A-' by the important rating agencies.

## CHARACTERISTICS OF THE PROPORTIONAL REINSURANCE

***a. Beginning/Duration:***

Reinsurance protection is usually bought for 12 months according to the financial year of the insurance company. Most trade credit insurers follow the period from 1 January to 31 December but a few buy protection starting in April or July. The duration is defined as either annually, i.e. the treaty will last for 12 months, or unlimited. In the former case, the reinsurance treaty has to be formally renewed before its expiry. In the latter case, the treaty will simply continue with the same conditions.

Renewal of reinsurance treaties is a two-step procedure: In the first step, the trade credit insurer will send a renewal information 'package' directly or via intermediaries to the reinsurers. The purpose of this is to obtain indications of possible interest by reinsurers to participate at terms and conditions which still will have to be defined. Parallel to this, the trade credit insurer will engage in more detailed discussions with the reinsurer who is expected to take the largest share. This reinsurer is the 'leading' reinsurer. If the trade credit insurer and the leading reinsurer agree on the conditions, then the trade credit insurer will get back to the broader reinsurance market with the 'final' terms and conditions. What seems to be very easy can, however, result in very lengthy and difficult renewal negotiations lasting even until the last day of the expiring treaty! Although a multi-year treaty would seem to be the solution if stability is at the centre of reinsurance arrangements, nevertheless both parties seem to prefer to keep some room for yearly negotiations should the performance under the treaty adversely develop and if trends forward are unclear.

***b. Cession basis:***

What does 'cession basis' mean? This is a way to assign (book) premium and losses to the reinsurance cover, the same way as it is done in direct policies. Unlike other lines of insurance such as property, fire or other, in trade credit insurance the reinsurance treaty only mentions that it covers 'all policies written (issued or renewed) during the period of reinsurance cover'. So, the premiums related to the policies issued between, say, 01-Jan and 31-Dec are assigned to this reinsurance period, and the losses related to buyers covered under these policies are also assigned to the same reinsurance period. This principle is called 'underwriting year basis' or 'risks-attaching basis', as opposed to 'occurrence year' where premiums and losses are assigned and booked according to the date they 'occur'. The proportional credit reinsurance treaties are normally set up on an underwriting year/ risk attaching basis.

***c. Retention:***

As briefly mentioned in the introduction, the level and amount of reinsurance that the trade credit insurer is willing to buy depends on many factors. Trade credit insurers have traditionally started by retaining about 30% of their business, but as business grew over the years and balance sheets became stronger, the trade credit insurer might decide to retain up to 70%. Figures will differ from one trade credit insurer to another. Of course, keeping a higher share of business without reinsurance significantly exposes a trade credit insurer's balance sheet, so it has become common in this line of business to protect this retained share with additional reinsurance protection. Usually such additional protection will be provided by the same reinsurers who are already participating in the proportional reinsurance treaty but there's no regulation requiring this and, in fact, some trade credit insurers might prefer to offer the retention protection to other reinsurers.

***d. Capacity:***

The definition of capacity or 'sum insured' is rather complex. In usual insurance terminology, a 'risk' is the deviation from an expected outcome. In trade credit insurance, a 'risk' is understood to be the buyer under a trade credit insurance policy. So, the reinsurance treaty protects against all risks, i.e. against the default of any buyer which is covered under any of the trade credit insurance policies issued by the trade credit insurer. As it is unlikely that all buyers in an insured portfolio would default or go bankrupt at the same time, the capacity under a reinsurance treaty will be set to cover the largest buyer exposure in the portfolio of the trade credit insurer. How is such exposure determined? The trade credit insurer will segregate its portfolio and determine which buyer has the highest number of credit limits. Summing up all credit limits on a per buyer group basis will then lead to knowing on which buyer the trade credit insurer is most exposed and how much reinsurance protection needs to be bought. Trade credit insurers will generally use the sum of granted credit limits rather than the sum of just used credit limits. With this information, the reinsurer will then define the reinsurance capacity per buyer in the treaty as the sum of all credit limits at 'any one time on any one buyer'. It is important to distinguish that, while the reinsurance treaty covers only policies issued during the period of the reinsurance cover, the capacity refers to the sum of all valid/in force credit limits independent of the underwriting year. So the capacity is not a capacity related to one specific underwriting year.

***e. Risk:***
We have just seen that capacity is defined on a 'per buyer' basis. But what is a buyer? As briefly illustrated in the introduction, for reinsurance purposes it is important to define exactly who 'the buyer' is. Is it a single legal entity? Is it a group of entities? What actually is a group of entities? When does a trade credit insurer have to accumulate all buyers to a group of buyers? Reinsurance treaties sometimes give very extensive answers to these questions (e.g.: a 'group' definition clause), but will also allow for the trade credit insurer's discretion in cases of uncertainty of deciding what is a 'buyer'. It is not the reinsurer but it is the trade credit insurer that is the sole judge as to what constitutes a buyer, and the accumulation of credit limits relating to it.

***f. Compensation:***
As mentioned, the reinsurer pays a commission to the trade credit insurer as a contribution to their costs. In an uncertain economic environment, quite often the fixed commission is replaced by a sliding scale where the commission depends on the loss ratio of the trade credit insurer (low loss ratio – high commission/high loss ratio – low commission). If the trade credit insurer develops a high loss ratio then its costs will not be covered by the commission. With a low loss ratio the trade credit insurer benefits from a 'nicer' commission.

In lieu of a sliding scale there is often established a combination of fixed commission plus a profit commission.

Other measures for the reinsurer to control its results in a difficult economic environment include the introduction of a loss participation or a loss corridor or loss cap. With these measures the insurer is prepared to participate on the losses when the losses exceed the agreed pre-defined loss ratio.

***g. Cover:***

The reinsurance treaties normally cover domestic credit and export credit insurance in combination with political risks (short term) as well as factoring business. Most of the programmes cover whole turnover polices and excess of loss policies and sometimes also single risk transactions. There are also reinsurance programmes available covering mainly single risk transactions and/or mainly pure political risks and there is also a market for top-up covers.

***h. Exclusions:***

Most of the credit reinsurance treaties do not cover Financial Guarantees according to the ICISA definition:

'A financial Guarantee is understood as comprising any bond, guarantee, indemnity or insurance, covering financial obligations in respect of any type of loan, personal loan and leasing facility, granted by a bank/credit institution, financial institution or financier or issued and executed in favour of any person or legal entity in respect of the payment or repayment of borrowed money or any contract transaction or arrangement – the primary purpose of which is to raise finance or secure sums due in respect of borrowed money.' Mortgage and consumer credit are normally excluded, as well. The reinsurance treaties also often contain a war exclusion clause which includes also Riots, Force Majeure as well Nuclear Risks, etc.

***i. Important clauses:***

- Change of underwriting policy clause (it is important for the reinsurer to be informed if a ceding company is changing its underwriting policy).
- Change in law clause (a change in the law can have a significant influence on the evaluation of a portfolio – e.g. introduction of business rescue, etc.).

- Error and omission clause (errors and omission should be rectified right away).
- Right of inspection clause (reinsurers would like to have the opportunity to review underwriting and claims files).
- Follow the fortune clause. In a reinsurance contract, the ceding company paying the claim wants to be free from the worry that the reinsurer will refuse to pay because it disagrees with the way the claim was handled or will require a strict proof of every element of the claim. The presence of this clause gives the ceding company wide latitude, safe from the judgemental eye of the reinsurer, in how it investigates, evaluates and resolves claims. The purpose of the clause is to ensure swift, unimpeded reimbursement to the company. The follow the fortunes clause does not give the ceding company free rein. There are limits to the latitude and discretion given to the ceding company under the clause. The reinsurer, under custom and practice, is not required to reimburse if there has been fraud, collusion, bad faith or if a claim is not even arguably covered under the reinsured contract.

***j. The claims handling***

Claims handling normally stays with the trade credit insurer. However, the reinsurance treaties often include a claims corporation clause which allows the reinsurer to take part in the claims handling. In working with trade credit insurers in different countries, reinsurers can be helpful due to their claims experience gained over the years with their clients worldwide. The reinsurance treaties include a loss notification limit as well as a cash loss limit, which defines when the reinsurers have to be notified and when reinsurers have to pay a claim outside any normal cycle.

***k. Portfolio Information:***

In order to evaluate a portfolio of trade credit insurance, reinsurers need to know the following information:

- Names of the buyers with limits/exposures above a certain threshold including the corresponding risk code/scoring of the trade credit insurer if available.

- Industries/sectors where the buyers are active.
- Buyer exposures per band including the risk codes of trade credit insurance if available.
- Statistics about the scoring, i.e. how much risks are in which category/scoring scale
- Country exposures with the corresponding classifications/ratings.
- 'Triangle' statistics/underwriting year loss ratio statistics.
- Information about claims/claims statistics.
- Comment/development about overdue/delay in payments.
- Acceptance rate.
- Comments about the economic development.
- Strategy of the trade credit insurer.

## CHARACTERISTICS OF THE NON-PROPORTIONAL REINSURANCE

### *Introduction*

The reinsurance market covers in general two types of non-proportional reinsurance structures. The most common (excess of loss on retention) is related to the protection of the retained part of the proportional quota share reinsurance treaty.

In some cases, trade credit insurers do not buy proportional reinsurance cover at all but would rely on a pure non-proportional cover in excess of a defined amount called the priority or deductible (excess of loss on gross). The cover is called the layer and can be split into several layers. The amount of the reinsurance cover usually goes up to the maximum underwriting limit per risk.

Without any specification, the non-proportional cover is meant to indemnify during the reinsurance period one single claim exceeding the priority. Once the cover (layer) is exhausted there would be nothing left for the next claim exceeding the priority. To avoid such a situation, the reinsurance cover would include a contractual agreement allowing the insurance company to reinstate the reinsurance capacity for the initial reinsurance period against a reinstatement premium to be paid. The number of reinstatements can vary (e.g. several reinstatements for a first layer exceeding the priority; or one or nil for the top layer).

***a. Cession basis (underwriting year vs. occurrence year)***

The cession basis or attachment principles are the same for non-proportional reinsurance as for proportional reinsurance albeit only applicable to the allocation of losses.

Underwriting year means that claims are attached to the reinsurance treaty year where the insurance policy has been issued or renewed; in some cases it could also refer to the shipments delivered.

Occurrence year is referring to the year in which the claim is incurred. Consequently, the date of claim is something that has to be specified (e.g. date of notification or date of the insolvency).

***b. Claims definition***

Underwriting limits are generally defined in reinsurance treaties as the aggregated amount of limits per risk (buyer or group of buyers) gross of self-retention and/or maximum limit of indemnification per insurance policy.

The cover is applicable to the proportional share of any claim the insurance company is retaining from its proportional reinsurance cover as long as the claim amount exceeds the deductible (priority).

*Some important clauses:*

The Ultimate Net Loss clause specifies the amount of all losses indemnified by an excess of loss treaty (i.e. the sum of settled losses pursuant to the liability as defined in the different policies) including claim and legal expenses and after deduction of all salvages and recoveries. The salaries of the employees involved in claims management as well as the office expenses of the insurance companies are not included.

The Interlocking Clause is only applicable to non-proportional reinsurance treaties working on underwriting year basis and when a loss is affecting more than one underwriting year. This could happen in cases were several insured policies with different inception periods are affected by one and the same claim. This objective is to split and apportion a loss from a single occurrence between two or more reinsurance periods. For this purpose the deductible to be retained by the insurance company and the maximum liability to be paid the reinsurance cover shall be reduced to the same percentage as the loss settled for every underwriting year and is in proportion to the total loss.

***c. Premium calculation (experience-based vs. exposure-based pricing)***

The premium ceded is not the part of the premium corresponding to the sum reinsured (as would be the case under proportional reinsurance) but rather is defined as the percentage of the premium retained proportionally from the Quota Share treaty. This is called the subject premium income.

This percentage, or premium rate, is determined on the basis of either the historical losses that have or would have been exposed to the non-proportional treaty, or the calculated risks exposed to the non-proportional reinsurance cover.

***d. Portfolio information***

Typical information that would be requested for pricing purposes includes periodical gross exposures per risk in order to determine the exposure to the layer(s) as well all historical claims that had exposed or would currently be expected to expose the layer. During the year the insurance company has to report on a quarterly basis the updated risk exposures as well as all claims notified or settled that are exceeding, say, 50% of the priority/deductible.

## FACULTATIVE TRADE CREDIT REINSURANCE

Contrary to the reinsurance described in the preceding paragraph where the objective is to protect whole portfolios, the facultative reinsurance comes into play when there is a need to protect a single debtor or a special transaction. Facultative coverage is characterized by an individual structure and a separate panel of reinsurers.

The motivation and the necessity to look for this single protection is generally given when there is no coverage for this particular business under an existing reinsurance treaty. This can be because the requested capacity for this individual risk exceeds the maximum treaty capacity under the automatic treaty or it can be because the underlying product or transaction is not considered or is explicitly excluded in the corresponding treaty. Another motivation could be that there is simply no treaty in place; this is rarely the case as professional players who write credit insurance usually have a reinsurance treaty protecting their portfolio.

However, in the cases described above where the risk does not fit into the reinsurance treaty, it is not unusual to buy facultative protection. The most common way to protect an extraordinary risk is by requesting a special acceptance under the existing reinsurance programme. By this the existing treaty can be extended in terms of capacity and/or wording. Using this method of special acceptance is faster and easier than a facultative placement as the credit insurer in principle only needs the formal approval of the leading reinsurers to have this risk covered in the existing reinsurance programme.

Another advantage of the special acceptance is the fact that the risk is included into an existing portfolio with already predefined commission and cession levels. This means that no additional negotiation of reinsurance conditions is necessary. Apart from that, a special acceptance, contrary to a facultative treaty, does not require a separate administration and is therefore not causing additional costs for neither party.

But not in all cases can a special acceptance be granted under the existing reinsurance programme. This is the case when the requested capacity for a single debtor is simply too high and would heavily unbalance the existing reinsurance treaty. Additional capacity may be added, then, through facultative reinsurance. Other reasons for rejecting a special limit under an existing treaty could be an inadequate risk quality or an undesirable type of transaction. In the latter cases, however, it would likely also be difficult to find facultative capacity.

Contrary to the automatic capacity under an existing treaty, the facultative treaty gives the reinsurer the possibility to offer a wider range of risk-sharing options according to the risk appetite it might have. For the insurer it is a good opportunity to attract and to test new reinsurance capacity that is not exposed via the existing treaty. For some reinsurers not participating in the existing treaty, it may be an interesting opportunity to establish a reinsurance relationship with the insurer.

Generally there is no separate active facultative reinsurance market for trade credit, as it may exist in other lines of insurance. Facultative reinsurance capacity in trade credit insurance is typically considered as a service product offered by the same automatic treaty reinsurers.

Technically, it is easier to place a separate/individual transaction on a facultative basis than by covering the transaction under an existing treaty. This is because the separate/individual transaction is a closed and clearly identifiable operation with specific exposures and premium income.

Buying additional capacity for a large debtor (buyer) via a proportional facultative treaty will raise the problem of correct premium allocation. As mentioned, the overall accumulation on a debtor usually is the sum of many individual credit lines granted to different policyholders. Thus it is already complicated to identify the premium corresponding to one single debtor in one whole turnover policy, a problem that is magnified by the purchase of additional capacity.

One way to solve this issue is by separating the exposure from the corresponding original premium income. The reinsurer would not seek a proportional participation in the underlying premium for this debtor, but would rather charge a fixed individual capacity premium that would be independent from the actual usage. The price has to be negotiated case by case with the trade credit insurer depending on the risk quality of the debtor. Protection can then be proportional or via a facultative Excess of Loss treaty.

Another method to avoid the premium allocation issue is to buy facultative capacity not only for a large debtor under a credit insurance policy but also for the whole credit insurance policy itself. Premium allocation would be easy as the facultative reinsurer would share an equal part of exposure and income.

The disadvantage of this procedure is that the credit insurer gives a substantial part of its premium income away to the facultative reinsurer with probably less favourable conditions compared to the existing treaty. At the same time, the facultative reinsurer not only has to release capacity for one single debtor, but for all debtors covered under the particular policy. Due to the dynamics of a credit insurance policy, the composition of the facultative book would be constantly changing requiring continuous reporting and information exchange.

The above-mentioned facts, as well as the concentration that the credit insurance market underwent in the last decade, have led to a substantial decrease in facultative requests in this line of business today. The existing programmes are generally designed so that large capacities for certain debtors can be obtained by special approval of the existing reinsurers. This procedure offers more flexibility to the credit insurers and allows them to quickly react to policyholder requirements.

# Trade Credit Insurance Resources

*This list contains books and publications on trade credit insurance ICISA is aware of. This list is not intended to be exhaustive and there may be other books and publications available.*


- Credit Insurance as an Anticyclical Tool. The Case of Spain Since 1970. (Spanish Title: *El Seguro De Credito Como Herramienta Anticyclica El Caso De Espana Desde 1970).* PhD by **Miguel Aguirre Uzquiano** (in Spanish) (2005)
- Research Report 03F07 Insurability of export credit risks. By **K. J. Alsem, J. Antufjew, K. R. E. Huizingh, R. H. Koning, E. Sterken and M. Woltil**
- Reference Guide to Reinsurance (2010). By **Albert P. Amato**
- Consumer Attitudes Toward Credit Insurance (Innovations in Financial Markets and Institutions). By **John M. Barron and Michael E. Staten**
- L'assurance-crédit dans la perspective de l'acte Unique de 1993 ce qu'elle est aujourd'hui et ce quelle sera. By **Jean Bastin**
- World Credit Insurance 2002. By **BCR Publishing**
- Handboek kredietverzekeringen. By **Paul Becue** (2008)

- Kredietverzekering – Mijn bedrijf goed verzekerd?! By **Paul Becue** (2011)
- Credit Insurance. How To Reduce The Risks Of Trade Credit. (1988) By **Dick Briggs and Burt Edwards**
- Trade Finance in Crisis, Market Adjustment or Market Failure? By **Jean-Pierre Chauffour and Thomas Farole** (published by the World Bank; July 2009)
- Trade Finance in Crisis, Should Developing Countries Establish Export Credit Agencies? By **Jean-Pierre Chauffour, Christian Saborowski and Ahmet I. Soylemezoghu** (published by the World Bank; January 2010)
- Power and Plenty: Trade, War and the World Economy in the Second Millennium, Princeton University Press. By **Ronald Findlay, Kevin H. O'Rourke** (2007)
- The Geneva Papers on Risk and Insurance. By **The Geneva Association** (January 2003)
- Export Credit Agencies. The Unsung Giants of International Trade and Finance. By **Delio E. Gianturco** (2001)
- Handbook of International Trade and Finance: The Complete Guide to Risk Management, international Payments and Currency Management, Bonds and Guarantees, Credit Insurance and Trade Finance. By **Anders Grath** (2008)
- (a publication, not a book:) ECA's and the License to Finance (in European ECA Reform Campaign). By **Nick Hildyard** (September 2006)
- Study on short-term trade finance and credit insurance in the European Union . By **International Financial Consulting Ltd.** for the European Commission (February 2012)
- 'Panorama des risques financiers spécifiques aux entreprises'. N° 55. Revue de la banque. By **Jacques Janssen** (1991)
- Trade Credit Insurance – Primer Series on Insurance Issue 15 (February 2010). By **Peter M. Jones**
- International Economics: Theory and Policy (1988). By **P. R. Krugman and M. Obstfeld**

- Trade and Trade Finance Developments in 14 Developing Countries Post September 2008. By **Mariem Malouche** (published by the World Bank; November 2009)
- Inter-Firm Trade Finance in Times of Crisis. By **Anna Maria C. Menchini** (published by the World Bank; November 2009)
- Die Kreditversicherung (1997). By **Bernd H. Meyer**
- Life of Adam Smith. New York City: Macmillan Publishers (1895). By **John Rae**
- Credit Insurance in Europe, Impact, Measurement & Policy Recommendations. By **Amparo San José Riestra** (Centre For European Policy Studies; February 2003)
- The Changing Role of Export Credit Agencies. By **Malcolm Stephens** (IMF, 1999)
- Products Offering Credit Insurance Protection As Alternatives to Traditional Credit Insurance. Study by **Technical Sub-Committee of ICISA** (1998)
- Ideas: A History of Thought and Invention from Fire to Freud. New York: HarperCollins Publishers (2005). By **Peter Watson**
- The Arrangement on Officially Supported Export Credits
- www.berneunion.org
- ICISA Yearbook
- www.icisa.org
- www.trademap.org/open_access/Product_SelProduct_TS.aspx
- www.worldshops.org/fairtrade/netw.html

## OTHER TRADE CREDIT INSURANCE ASSOCIATIONS:

- The International Union of Credit & Investment Insurers (Berne Union)
  www.berneunion.org
- The Latinamerican Association of Export Credit Insurance Organisms (ALASECE)
  www.alasece.com

# Glossary of Trade Credit Terminology

# TERMS BY CATEGORY

## CLAIMS/INDEMNITY

***Adverse information***
Events or circumstances that have led or may lead to a deterioration in the financial situation or creditworthiness of a buyer or a country of a buyer.

***Aggregate first loss (AFL, Policy deductible)***
The total amount of approved claims during an insurance period, which are to be borne by the insured for their own account prior to indemnification by the insurer.

***Claim (Notice of claim)***
An application by the insured for indemnification of a loss under the policy.

***Claims made policy***
A policy which covers applications for indemnification made during the policy term.
*See also losses occurring policies and risk attaching policy*

***Claims threshold (Non-qualifying loss, Threshold)***
The amount below which losses do not qualify for indemnification and are to be kept by the insured for their own account.

***Claims waiting period (Claim filing waiting period, Waiting period)***
The period, usually starting from the due date of payment or intervention order, after the expiry of which a claim may be submitted and the loss is assessed.

***Costs for work in progress (Pre-invoicing expenses, Costs incurred but not billed)***
Expenses incurred for uncompleted rendered services or product construction.

***Date of ascertainment of loss (Date of loss)***

1. Date on which the insured loss will be assessed by the insurer;
2. date on which the insured loss is deemed to have occurred.

***Datum line***

An amount below which buyers are not to be included in the insurance policy.

***Default (Payment default)***

The failure of the buyer to meet their contractual (payment) obligations. A default is an event that can lead to a loss for the credit insurer, such as bankruptcy, Chapter 11 (or any other failure to pay of the buyer) which is covered under the insured's policy.

***Imminent loss***

Any events or circumstances that have led or may lead to a high possibility of a claim.

***Indemnification***

Compensation for a loss.

***Minimum retention***

The minimum amount of each loss that the insured has to bear for their own account.

***Non-payment risk***

The risk that a buyer will default on its obligation to pay an invoice.

***Non-qualifying loss (Claims threshold, NQL, Threshold)***

The amount below which losses do not qualify for indemnification and are to be kept by the insured for their own account.

***Notice of claim (Claim)***

An application by the insured for indemnification of a loss under the policy.

***Repudiation (of cover)***
The decision of the insurer not to accept a specific claim made by the insured due to

1. a breach of obligation by the insured;
2. the underlying risk being outside the scope of coverage under the respective policy.

***Rescheduling***
Amending the credit terms of a debt by setting one or more new due dates.

***Subrogation***
Upon payment or indemnification of a claim to the insured caused by a failure of the buyer, the insurer steps into the insured's position and assumes all rights and remedies of the insured against the buyer. By executing these rights and remedies the insurer can

1. possibly recover the indemnified amount from the buyer;
2. avoid overcompensation to the insured.

Subrogation occurs without any agreement between the insurer and the insured.

## CREDIT ASSESSMENT/LIMITS

***Aggregate limit (Policy limit, Insurer's maximum liability, Maximum Sum Insured)***
The maximum amount that the insurer is liable to pay in respect of all losses during a policy period.

***Blind cover***
A policy feature that provides (a reduced percentage of) cover when no credit limit has been established on the buyer and no adverse information is known.
*See also under First sale clause/First order cover.*

***Credit assessment fee (Credit rating fee)***
Contribution to the costs of credit information gathered for the assessment of the buyer's risk.

***Credit limit***
The maximum exposure specifically approved or otherwise authorised by the insurer in respect of a buyer.

***Credit underwriting (Limit underwriting)***
Assessment by the credit insurer of the financial condition of buyers, before setting a credit limit.

***Discretionary limit (DL, Discretionary credit limit, DCL, Non-vetting limit)***
The amount up to which, according to given guidelines, the insured may set a credit limit without specific review by the insurer.

***First order cover (First sale clause)***
A policy feature that provides cover for risks commencing before a credit limit has been established, for buyers with whom the insured has not traded before.

***Grace period***
In general, a length of time during which rules, actions, obligations or penalties are deferred. In short term turnover credit insurance typically used to describe a period between the announcement and actual effective date of credit limit reductions or withdrawals.

***Non-cancellable limits***
Credit limits which remain valid for the duration of the policy period and cannot be cancelled by the insurer. Cover, however, may be automatically deactivated on the occurrence of certain defined events, e.g. rating downgrade, overdue payments, etc.

***Partial acceptance of a limit***

The decision of an underwriter not to grant in full the credit limit amount applied for by the insured.

## FINANCIAL AND EXPORT TERMS

***Discharge of debt***

Relief of a party from a financial commitment.

***Factoring***

Factoring is a financial transaction whereby a business transfers all or a large part of its accounts receivable to a third party (called the factor) at a discount in exchange for immediate cash. Factoring is typically suitable for open account sales with short-term (up to 180 days) credit periods, for both domestic and international trade. Factoring may be done on a recourse or a non-recourse basis.

***Forfaiting***

Forfaiting is a financial transaction whereby a business sells a single or a series of single account receivables to a third party (called the forfaitor) at a discount in exchange for immediate cash. Forfaiting is typically oriented at sales involving negotiable instruments (bills of exchange or promissory notes) with long credit periods (more than 180 days) and for export business only. Forfaiting is done on a non-recourse basis.

***Irrevocable (documentary) letter of credit***

1. Unalterable obligation of a bank authorizing a person or company to draw money up to a specified amount, usually a third party bank, subject to documentary compliance.
2. As per definition in UPC.

## GENERAL TERMS

***Assignee (Loss payee)***

A party to whom (by authorization of the insured) the legal rights to a claim payment under a policy is transferred

***Broker (Agent)***
The party via whom an application for insurance is presented from prospective insured to the insurer.

***Buyer (Debtor)***
The business entity to which an insured sells their goods or services.

***Client (Insured, Policyholder)***
The party that purchases the insurance policy has the right of all benefits of the policy and assumes responsibilities and obligations under that policy.

***Commission***
Remuneration of a party (e.g. a broker for services rendered).

***Commissioning***
Quality control process to ensure that a contract or project is performed, completed and fully operational in accordance with the agreed requirements, design, plan or specifications, e.g. in the building industry, shipbuilding industry, machine construction sector.

***Concessional loan***
A loan granted on terms more generous than prevailing market terms (e.g. lower interest rate, longer repayment period, longer grace period)

***Credit insurance***
Credit insurance or trade credit insurance covers the payment risk resulting from the delivery of goods and services on credit terms.

***Customer (Buyer, Debtor, Insured, Policyholder)***
'Customer' may refer to both the buyer and the insured.
*See under these terms.*

***Endorsement (Policy clause)***
An addendum or enhancement to the policy conditions.

***Facultative (re)insurance (FAC)***
(Re)insurance in respect of a particular risk instead of a portfolio of risks.

***Financial Guarantee***
A Financial Guarantee is understood as comprising any bond, guarantee, indemnity or insurance, covering financial obligations in respect of any type of loan, personal loan and leasing facility, granted by a bank/credit institution, financial institution or financier or issued or executed in favour of any person or legal entity in respect of the payment or repayment of borrowed money or any contract transaction or arrangement – the primary purpose of which is to raise finance or secure sums due in respect of borrowed money.

By way of explanation, the purpose of this definition is the avoidance of insurance cover for any financial obligation which does not arise from or relates to a trade transaction defined as the supply of goods and/or rendering of services.

***Insured (Policyholder, Client, Named insured, Primary insured)***
The party that purchases the insurance policy and assumes responsibilities and obligations under the policy.

***Insured transaction (Insured obligation, Insured buyer obligation)***
An obligation owing from a specific buyer to the insured and falling within the scope of the insurance contract.

***Insurer***
The party offering insurance policies for premiums, an underwriter.

***Joint insurance***
Insurance offered by more than one insurer for their combined account.

***Joint insured (Additional named insured, Co-insured)***
A party which together with the insured purchases the insurance policy and assumes specified responsibilities and obligations.

***Joint insurer***
An insurer offering insurance policies in cooperation with one or more other insurers for their combined account.

***Lien***
The broadest term for any sort of charge or encumbrance against or a security interest granted over an item of property that secures the payment of a debt or performance of some other obligation. The owner of the property, who grants the lien, is referred to as the lienee and the person who has the benefit of the lien is referred to as the lienor.

***Main insured***
The leading insured acting on behalf of a group of joint-insured.

***Main insurer***
The leading insurer acting on behalf of a group of joint insurers.

***Non-binding indication (NBI, Quotation non-binding, Quote non-binding)***
An insurer's written offer of policy terms and conditions, subject to change by the insurer.

***Offer of cover***
An indication of conditions for cover based on information given on an application form.

***Open account***
An open account transaction is a sale where the goods are shipped and delivered before payment is due, which is usually in 30 to 90 days. Obviously, this option is advantageous to the buyer in terms of cash flow and cost, but it contains consequently a non-payment risk for the supplier

***Policy currency***
The currency in which all financial transactions or amounts under the policy are denominated (credit limits, indemnifications, costs, premium, deductibles, etc.).

***Policyholder (Insured client)***

The party that purchases the insurance policy and assumes responsibilities and obligations under the policy.

***Probable Maximum Loss (PML)***

The anticipated maximum loss potential in the total exposure. In credit insurance, this is impacted by the credit insurer's ability to work down their exposure before the buyer default and their risk management and recovery technique after the buyer default. To calculate the PML, the following data are used: credit limit one year before the buyer default, credit limit at time of buyer default and ultimate loss amount.

***Renewal***

The prolongation of a policy or a credit limit after the expiry of their validity or after a specified period of time.

## INSURABLE DEBTORS

***Guarantor***

An individual or company that gives a promise or assurance that an obligation owing from the buyer to the insured will be paid.

***Key debtor or cover for key debtor (Key buyer, Key customer, Major Debtor Cover)***

(Cover for) the insured's largest buyers only (as opposed to whole turnover cover or single risk cover).

***Private buyer (Private debtor)***

The business entity to which an insured sells its goods or services and that is

1. not a public buyer;
2. not majority-owned by a government.

***Private individual***

A person who buys goods or services for a purpose other than the purpose of their professional activity or business.

***Public buyer (Government buyers, Government debtors)***
The entity to which an insured sells its goods or services and that is

1. authorised to enter into commitments in the name or on behalf of the government of its country, including the government itself, government agencies or any public sector institutions;
2. majority-owned by a government;
3. an entity whose commitments are guaranteed by the government.

## INSURABLE DEBTORS/CREDIT ASSESSMENT

***Unspecified customer (DCL buyer/debtor, Unnamed buyer/debtor)***
A buyer for which, according to given guidelines, the insured may set a credit limit without specific review by the insurer.

## INSURANCE COVER

***Binding order (Binding contracts)***
An order from which the insured cannot be released if the buyer's financial soundness is deteriorating. Under pre-defined conditions, credit insurance may be offered for such contracts even after withdrawal of the credit limit.

***Co-insurance (Uninsured percentage, Self-insured percentage, Retention, Retained risk)***
The percentage of each insured loss that is not indemnified by the insurer and that the insured has to bear for its own account.

***Commencement of cover (Transaction date)***
The date on which the insurance begins to take effect (at date of order or transaction, delivery or shipment, completion of performance of services) for each individual trade transaction covered under the policy.

***Commercial risk***
The risk of a deterioration in the financial situation or creditworthiness of a private buyer, resulting in payment default by or the insolvency of the buyer, not caused by circumstances or occurrences defined as political risk.

***Comprehensive cover***

1. Insurance covering the entire sales turnover of the insured (opp. Single risk cover);
2. insurance for both commercial and political risks.

***Consignment***
Possession of goods by a consignee with the obligation to pay the supplier after the sale to a third party or when using the goods.

***Covered percentage (Insured percentage, Percentage of cover, Percentage of indemnification, Guaranteed percentage, Indemnity amount)***
The percentage of each insured loss that is indemnified by the insurer.

***Deductible***
The amount of loss that must be absorbed by the insured before indemnification under the policy.

***Delivery***
Making the goods available to the buyer or any person acting on their behalf at the place and on the terms specified in the sales contract.

***Each and every first loss***
The amount to be deducted from each claim payment to be kept for the account of the insured.

***Effective date (of the policy)***
The date on which the policy comes into force.

***Export credit insurance***
Insurance against the credit risk related to the sale of goods to buyers in another country.

***Losses occurring policy***
A policy under which cover is conditional on the date of the cause of loss occurring within the policy period.
*See also Risk Attaching policy and Claims Made policy.*

***Manufacturing period***
The period between the date of order and the delivery or shipment of the goods.

***Maximum liability (Policy limit, Aggregate limit, Insurer's maximum liability, Maximum Sum Insured)***
The maximum amount that the insurer is liable to pay in respect of all losses during a policy period.

***Percentage of cover (Insured percentage, Guaranteed percentage, Covered percentage, Percentage of indemnification)***
The percentage of each insured loss that is indemnified by the insurer.

***Policy limit (Aggregate limit, Annual maximum liability, Maximum Sum Insured)***
The maximum amount that the insurer is liable to pay in respect of all losses during a policy period.

***Retained risk***
The part of a loss which is not indemnified by the insurer and for which the insured must bear the loss without recourse to any other party.

***Retention of title (ROT, Reservation of title)***
A condition in a sales contract which reserves the seller's right of product ownership until the seller has received full payment.

***Risks Attaching policy***
A policy under which cover attaches based on shipment dates and where the shipment date (but not necessarily the loss) must occur within the policy period.
*See also Claims made policy, Losses occurring policy.*

***Run off cover***
Continuation of cover of risks, where the cover commenced before withdrawal of a credit limit or the expiry of a policy until payment or until the occurrence of a covered cause of loss.

***Run-in cover***
Inclusion of cover of amounts outstanding on buyers at the effective date of the policy or the date a credit limit applied for or established.

***Single buyer cover (Single debtor/Single risk cover, Transactional cover, Specific Account)***
Cover for all sales to one debtor or for a single contract with one debtor (as opposed to whole turnover and key buyer).

***Third country risk***
Exposure to economic and political risks in a country other than the country of the insured or of the buyer; usually a country through which shipments may pass or where the goods are to be delivered, or the services to be performed.

***Top-up cover (Excess insurance)***
Additional coverage over a credit limit established by the same or another insurer.

***Uninsured percentage (Co-insurance, Retained risk, Retention, Self-insured percentage)***
The percentage of each insured loss that is not indemnified by the insurer and that the insured has to bear for their own account.

***Whole turnover policy***
A credit insurance policy that covers the insured's total credit sales (as opposed to Key buyer cover and Single risk cover).

INSURANCE COVER/FINANCIAL AND EXPORT TERMS

***Shipment***
The placement en route to the buyer of the goods ordered by the buyer.

INSURED DEBTS/TURNOVER

***Accounts payable***
Amounts owed by a company from the purchase of goods and services on credit terms.

***Accounts receivable***
Amounts due to a company from the sale of goods and services on credit terms.

***Credit term (Credit period, Payment term)***
1. The period after delivery or shipment of goods or after rendering of services at the expiry of which invoices are due to be paid.
2. The period of time provided by the insured to the buyer for repayment of delivered goods or services.

***Delivery period***
The period between date of order and delivery or shipment of goods.

***Domestic business***
Transactions with buyers domiciled in the same country as the insured.

***Due date***
Date by which the buyer must pay their debt according to the sales contract or invoice.

***Extension of due date (Due date extension, Deferral of payment)***
Granting of a credit term longer than originally agreed upon in the sales contract.

***Extension period (Maximum extension period)***
The maximum due date extension allowed under a policy.

***Maximum credit terms (Maximum payment terms)***
The longest credit period approved for a buyer under the policy.

***Maximum pre-credit risk period***
The maximum insured period between contract date and shipment of goods or provision of services.

***Mean delivery date***
Average period between date of order and date of delivery or shipment of goods or completion of services.

***Mean length of credit***
Average period between delivery or shipment of goods and due date of invoice.

***Medium-term business***
Transactions under which the insured provides the buyer with a credit period between 1 and 3 to 5 years in length, usually characterised by a down payment followed by equal installment payments.

***Payment term (Credit period, Credit term)***
1. The period after delivery or shipment of goods or after rendering of services at the expiry of which invoices are due to be paid.
2. The period of time provided by the insured to the buyer for payment for delivered goods or services.

***Short-term business***
Transactions under which the insured provides the buyer with a credit period up to two years.

***Tenor***
Length of the risk period (the period that the credit insurer is on risk)

## INSURED RISKS

***Act of State***
A law, decision or action by a sovereign state that cannot be questioned or redressed by the courts of another state. An Act of State may prevent or frustrate the performance or completion of a credit-insured trade contract or transaction.

***Contract frustration***
Impossibility to perform a trade contract.

***Contract repudiation***
An arbitrary withdrawal of a party from its duties and responsibilities imposed by a contract.

***Contract risk***
The commercial risk of insolvency of a buyer before delivery or shipment of the goods or performance of a service, and/or the political risk of any interruption of the manufacturing of the goods or performance of a service.

***Conversion and transfer risk (Transfer risk)***
1. The risk of revocation by the buyer's government of the buyer's pre-existing legal right to make payment in an invoiced currency other than the currency of the buyer country, at any rate of exchange.
2. Political risk resulting from an event outside the insured's country preventing or delaying the transfer of funds paid by the debtor to a local bank.

***Country cover conditions***
Terms of coverage imposed by the insurer for their acceptance of cover on (buyers in) a particular country.

***Country limit***
The maximum exposure specifically approved or otherwise authorised by the insurer in respect of a particular country.

***Country rating (Country rank, Country risk classification)***
An indication of creditworthiness of a country.

***Exchange risk***
Fluctuation in the buyer's currency against another currency, which may affect the buyer's financial ability to pay its obligations.

***Expropriation***
The act of a government taking property away from its owner(s).

***Fait du Prince***
French term to describe an action taken unilaterally by the government of a country. A Fait du Prince may prevent or frustrate the performance or completion of a credit-insured trade contract or transaction.

***Insolvency (Bankruptcy)***
A judicial or administrative procedure whereby the assets and affairs of the buyer are made subject to control or supervision by the court or a person or body appointed by the court or by law, for the purpose of reorganization or liquidation of the buyer or of the rescheduling, settlement or suspension of payment of its debts.

***Moratorium***
A cessation of payments, usually by a government, to all or a class of creditors.

***Natural disasters (Acts of God)***
The manifestation of a natural force that is beyond the control of the insured, buyer, guarantor or government.
*See also Political risk.*

***Non-acceptance of goods***
The refusal or failure of the buyer to take possession of products shipped by the insured.

***Payment default (Default)***
The failure by a buyer to make payment for delivered goods or services by the due date specified in the invoice or sales contract. A default is an event that could lead to a loss for the credit insurer such as bankruptcy, Chapter 11, (or any other failure to pay of the buyer) which is covered under the insured's policy.

***Political risk (Country risk)***

1. The risk that a government buyer or country prevents the fulfillment of a transaction or fails to meet payment obligations in time.
2. A risk that is beyond the scope of an individual buyer or falls outside the individual buyer's responsibility.
3. The risk that a country prevents the performance of a transaction.
4. The risk that a country remains in default to transfer to the country of the insured the moneys paid by buyers domiciled in that country.

***Post-shipment risk***
The risk of non-payment arising after the delivery of shipment of the goods or completion of the performance of services.

***Pre-credit risk (Pre-shipment risk, Work in process)***
The commercial risk of insolvency of a buyer before delivery or shipment of the goods or performance of a service, and/or the political risk of any interruption of the manufacturing of the goods or performance of a service.

***Protracted default (Default)***

The failure by a buyer to pay the contractual debt within a pre-defined period calculated from the due date or extended due date of the debt.

***Transfer delay***

The period of time between a foreign buyer applying for foreign exchange to repay their obligation to an insured and the insured receiving the funds.

***Waiting period (Claim filing waiting period)***

The period, usually starting from the due date of payment or intervention order, after the expiry of which a claim may be submitted and the loss is assessed.

***War***

A declared military conflict between nations.

## OBLIGATIONS

***Arrears***

Alternative term for Overdue account. The term 'in arrears' is also used to refer to premium payments to be made at the end of a period (typically on the basis of the policyholder's declaration of invoiced turnover or outstanding balances for that period), as opposed to premium payments 'in advance', i.e. at the start of the relevant period.

***Duty to notify***

Obligation of the insured to notify the insurer of changes of insurable turnover as indicated on the applications form for the policy, adverse information oroverdue accounts.

***Overdue account (Past due account, Defaulted account)***

A buyer's obligation that has not been paid by its due date.

## PREMIUM/FEES

***Declaration of outstanding balances***

The specification of outstanding balances (typically at end of the month) on the buyers covered under the policy for the purpose of premium calculation.

***Declaration of turnover (Shipment report, Insured transactions report)***

The specification of the invoiced turnover on the buyers covered under the policy for the purpose of premium calculation.

***Deposit premium***

(Installments of) premium paid in advance, to be adjusted on receipt of the declaration of turnover or outstanding balances.

***Minimum premium***

The agreed minimum amount of premium to be paid for a specified period regardless of the volume of declared turnover or outstanding balances.

***No claims bonus (No claims credit, Low claims bonus)***

An amount or percentage provided to the insured as a reduction of premium owed, depending on the claims ratio of the policy.

***Premium***

The sum of money paid to buy an insurance product.

***Profit share***

1. An arrangement whereby the insured can receive back a portion of premiums paid according to certain conditions (usually dependent on the claim ratio of the policy).
2. The distribution of a percentage of the profits of the policy back to the insured according to certain conditions (usually dependent on the claim ratio of the policy).

## RECOVERY/DEBT COLLECTION

***Collateral***

Assets, rights or guarantees pledged as security by the buyer or by a third party on behalf of the buyer for the extension of credit by the insured to the buyer.

***Collections costs***

The costs incurred in preventing or minimizing the loss or in collection of the amount owed by the buyer.

***Recoveries (Salvage)***

Proceeds received from the buyer or a third party, whether before or after a claim has been indemnified.

***Salvage (Recoveries)***

Proceeds received from the buyer or a third party, whether before or after a claim has been indemnified.

## REINSURANCE/NEIGHBOURING TERMS

***Asset-backed securities***

Financing of companies by the capital market through commercial papers (securities), sold by a Special Purpose Vehicle to investors, backed by the debts (assets) sold to a Special Purpose Vehicle.

***Excess of loss (XL, XoL)***

Insurance, cover or indemnification in excess of an amount of first loss to be borne by the insured.

***Quota-share treaty***

Reinsurance in respect of a portfolio of risks insured by a primary insurer and under which the risk is shared on a percentage basis between the insurer and the reinsurer, i.e. not on an excess-of-loss basis.

## REPORTING TERMS

***Claims ratio***

Claims payments and expenses divided by gross earned premium and premium related revenue.

***Combined ratio***

1. The sum of claims payments, claims expenses and underwriting expenses, including the cost of credit information, divided by the sum of earned premium and premium related revenue.
2. The sum of claims ratio and underwriting expense ratio.

***Contingent liability***

A conditional obligation of one party to another, triggered by specified events.

***Cost ratio (Underwriting ratio, Expense ratio)***

The sum of underwriting expenses, including the cost of credit information, divided by the sum of earned premium, including premium-related revenue.

***Exposure***

The total amount underwritten by the insurer as cover on a buyer, a country or under a policy or all policies.

# ALPHABETICAL LIST OF ALL TERMS

www.ingramcontent.com/pod-product-compliance
Ingram Content Group UK Ltd.
Pitfield, Milton Keynes, MK11 3LW, UK
UKHW041829100926
8556IPUK00002B/93

9 781783 084821